about how to translate the vision and passion within her into an outward expression. Cherri Walston's ardent charge to women to become Chairwoman of their own lives is life-changing. This book is a must read for women who desire to abandon the self-debilitating behaviors and patterns of thinking which have precluded them from their divine appointment.

– Crystal Lee, *Chief Executive Office*
www.LEEdershipInstitute.org

I0111820

If you don't choose your purpose, path and destiny, someone else will choose it for you and you'll be living their vision instead of your own. If you know there is a deeper, more meaningful vision for your life beyond what you see in front of you, choose to start living your vision today. Cherri Walston has created a masterpiece blueprint to help you unleash, clarify and live the vision in your heart. *HER Exit Strategy* inspires you to create a vibrant vision for your life and empowers you to actualize it. If you are ready to escape the mediocrity of punching a clock, the mundane of settling for what you see, and doing meaningless work in your life, get *HER Exit Strategy* and take the leap into living your vision, doing what you love, and living a life that fulfills and excites you.

– **Catrice M. Jackson**, *Speaker, BOSSLady of Branding, and International Best-Selling Author*

Cheri Walston uses her own experiences, God-given talents, and *big vision* to inspire women to become all they were created to be. Through her inspired words, she calls women to take courageous action to live a fulfilling life of personal ownership, replacing fear with faith. Creating a vision, taking steps with confidence and a "can do" attitude, and living out an *Exit Strategy* are central themes that Cheri uses to challenge our thinking, our actions, and our journey.

– **Annette R. Knight**, *CHRO, SPHR*

Cherri Walston has a gift for pulling women out of the routine-ness of busy lives toward the passions that quietly brew in our hearts. Cherri writes in a voice that nearly every working woman can relate to, telling stories that resonate with us all. But her guidance doesn't end with feel good quotes and inspiration. She also leaves the reader with actionable steps that are truly the key to change and progress. Inspiration without action is just a daydream, but reading Ms. Walston's work effectively takes you from hopes and dreams to a clear vision of how you will pursue your entrepreneurial passions. I highly recommend Cherri Walston's book and coaching services to set you on the path to realizing your own entrepreneurial success.

– **LaShanda Brown**, NP, Ph.D.(c) *Certified Health Coach,*
  Good Healthy Roots Wellness Center

Cherri Walston has written a book that I wish I had in my hands before I started my entrepreneurial journey. It is informative and straightforward. You will be able to turn the pages of her book and develop an outstanding exit strategy. You will hear Cherri's care and concern as you delve into the book. She is truly a coach who has been custom designed to show you how to transition from working for someone else to working for yourself. I wholeheartedly endorse *HER Exit Strategy*. It is indeed a book that should be on bookshelves in homes, libraries and bookstores for years to come.

– **Stevii Aisha Mills**, *The SHE Suite*
  www.Stevii.com

In *HER Exit Strategy*, Cherri Walston has fashioned a gem by marrying the wisdom extracted from both her personal and professional experiences. The work's conversational tone makes the reader feel as if she is talking with a dear friend over coffee

HER EXIT STRATEGY

THE WORKING WOMAN'S
FREEDOM PLAN
TO LIVE YOUR BIG VISION

CHERRI WALSTON

purposely
created
PUBLISHING

HER Exit Strategy, 2nd Edition
Copyright © 2014 Cherri Walston

Published by: Purposely Created Publishing Group™

Printed in the United States of America

ISBN: 0-692-29474-0

ISBN-13: 978-0-692-29474-1

Special discounts are available on bulk quantity purchases by book clubs, associations and special interest groups. For details email: Sales@PublishYourGift.com or call (866) 674-3340.

For more information, log onto
www.PublishYourGift.com

DEDICATION

This book is dedicated in loving memory of my dearest friend, Jocelyn Hollowell, who inspired me to reach for the stars. She left a lasting legacy and impression on my heart for the joy of life and taught me to never stop striving for the best. I still feel her spirit guiding me and encouraging me to go for it. I love and miss her dearly.

To my mother, Evelyn Walston, who is the most courageous and victorious woman I know, had a vision for a better life and pursued it. Thank you for being a role model for what a woman can achieve when she puts her mind to it.

To the most amazing brother a sister could ever wish for, James Walston: You have been like the captain of my ship, helping me navigate and find my way when I wasn't sure where I needed to go. You've always believed in me, encouraged me, and I am blessed to be your big sister.

To my nieces, Jamie and Jayla, and nephews, Jaden and Justice, I'm proud to be your Aunt ReeRee!

CONTENTS

FOREWORD BY BECKY A. DAVIS

Every professional woman needs an exit strategy. What is an exit strategy? It's a well-thought out tactical plan that prepares you for making your next career move and gives you control over your career and life, no matter what happens next. Companies wouldn't allow a division, department, or company to simply run along aimlessly without a forward-focused business plan that includes several contingency scenarios. The same should be true for you. If you don't have an exit strategy, you're effectively abandoning control of your life and career, leaving your future flapping in the wind.

After the economic downturn in 2008, the realization set in that you could have a job today and it could be gone tomorrow. Are you prepared if you lost your job tomorrow? Most people are not.

Only 4.8% of Fortune 500 CEOs are women, though women have been consistently launching businesses at nearly twice the rate of men. As important, their growth in employment and revenues has continued to outpace the economy. Women-owned businesses are already serious players in this nation's economy.

So many women hate their jobs and would love to start their own business, but they are afraid because they don't know where to start or even *how* to start. I worked in Corporate America for over 20 years, but always had a desire to live my dreams of speaking and motivating people all over the world. It wasn't until my company got a new CEO and I started working for another one of our brands that I saw an unfamiliar shift in the culture. It was a shift that created an environment where people quite often felt threatened of losing their jobs. The values of the organization started to go out the window. At that time, I started to put some thought into what my next move would be. Things got really bad and I began to work on my exit strategy to prepare myself for the next chapter of my life and live my big vision.

In this book, Cherri will give you a clear picture of what to expect when you begin your exit strategy and she is right on point because I experienced it all.

This book will help you gain insight, skills and a freedom plan to live your big vision. Living your big vision will change your life. Take it from me, I'm living my big vision and after reading this book, I hope you'll join me.

Becky A. Davis

INTRODUCTION

Every smart, working and professional woman should have an exit strategy which creates an open door that removes her from any opposing mindset, behavior, life, or career event hindering her from living the life she deserves, desires and that's divinely designed for her. **HER Exit Strategy** is a *vision* comprised of a well-thought out, tactical plan that prepares her for making her next steps that gives her control over her life no matter what happens next. An exit is a choice we all can create when faced with life situations, unpleasantries, beliefs, and behaviors that block our paths to a life we envision for the present and future.

As women, we have the loving tendency to support others' dreams and visions, but leave ours to chance. Hoping and waiting for the best without a plan to navigate our course. Corporate America still hasn't fully recognized women and their beautiful minds and abilities as leaders and change agents, yet we allow them to control our destiny. We offer them our gifts and talents without realizing our own worth as precious gems hidden and only used for special occasions (overtime). Instead of fulfilling our deep desires for what's yearning and calling us to live on the inside, we become comfortable and conform to what our jobs, careers and other people think we need to do, be and have as a template for what's best for us.

We can easily get swiped up in our day-to-day lives and live without any direction or meaning but going to work and doing a good job. Where is the joy in the mundane? Where is the joy in operating on rote with no passion? Where is the joy in following someone else's vision and being blind to your own divine path? Where is the joy in being frozen with fear and not living in the greatness of your gifts? Where is the joy in having a great idea that will make a difference and not take it on the test drive of entrepreneurship? There's no joy; it's a trap without an exit route! Inside of every woman, there is a dream and vision waiting to exhale in a world with unlimited possibilities. However, she needs to escape into this new way of living and being with an *exit strategy* that releases her from all the "doorstoppers" which block her path to living her biggest, wildest God-inspired vision that only *she* can co-create with a freedom plan to live her big vision.

This book has been in my *big vision* container that's held all of my dreams and desires for several years now. It's one of those visions that's been trapped by my own mind-trap and the viewpoints of others, who may have thought they had my best interest at heart. I'm writing this book for two reasons: to live my exit strategy in a way that gets my message out to professional, aspiring entrepreneurial women in the world and to give you, the reader, a freedom plan to create your exit strategy—one that will swing open the door with a vision beneath your wings to live a vibrant life. I've coached and crossed paths with too many women in the workplace who don't have a vision for their own life. Consequently, they become victims of a cubicle cell waiting for the guards to release them for a couple of hours of light at designated times. Some have also surrendered total control over their destiny, expecting a fair reward for their time, energy and effort. This pains me and I have felt compelled to help women create a personal vision for their lives, one that will move them beyond their perceived limitations. It's possible—I'm doing it and that's why I'm excited about writing it!

This book is about kicking down the door and creating an exit out of the "stuff" that keeps you from living the life you were meant to have and were divinely created for. It is about being unstoppable with courageous confidence to take action on your own behalf to design the life you've been putting off because of your outer vision circumstances (stuff that keeps you stuck, trapped and hiding your greatness). I'm giving you the plan and the permission to run through the open door with a strategy to free yourself from the 9-to-5 mindset and take ownership of your authentic journey.

I've had to escape my own issues that were holding me hostage me from living the vision I held for my life. I've had many life events—personal and professional—that tried to block my path from being the extraordinary woman I know God created me to be. The biggest life-altering challenge was my eyesight. Being told that I may lose my eyesight and watching it slowly change and narrow into tunnel vision was like groping in the dark, but a flicker of inner light kept me from totally losing my footing. Although my outer vision was slightly diminishing, my *inner vision* was calling me to something greater than the perceived limitations of why I couldn't have a vibrant life. My initial exit strategy was to learn how to change my view to see unlimited possibilities that were waiting for me on the other side of the door. I never played the victim of circumstances card but the victorious card of a woman who had much determination to free herself from anything that blocked peace, joy, happiness, and the vision. I've had to make a mass exodus out of an unhealthy marriage and relationships, break free from jobs that didn't express or enhance my natural skill set, and hear the inner critics rantings while allowing my inner vision to muffle the deafening sounds and believe that if I couldn't use my gifts or have them valued in the workplace, there would be a marketplace for my passion.

Even during those times, I felt myself shrinking and hiding my light, yet I always found myself helping others step into their spotlight. I'm a true guiding light, and when I trust and allow myself to be in that space, my inner and outer being is full of GLOW. I get to live my big vision life by showing others how to live their vision. It's interesting how God gave me the gift of struggle with my own eyesight, only to create a platform to empower others to create and live their vision for what they want for theirs. Notice I implied my struggle as a gift; I choose to see things as a way to empower me to shape something meaningful out of what could be perceived as a limitation. Big visions should never be about your limitations to attaining what you want, but gravitating towards what's awaiting you in the horizon.

Are you ready to get clear and be free to live your big vision life?

Then this book will show you how to break free and step out with a freedom plan to take control of your life with simple, action-oriented steps to make your personal dream and vision a reality. This book has two parts that will guide you into creating a plan for your personal and business vision:

"The Escape Route for Your Big Vision Life" will give you the keys to unlock the chains of life that keeps you in bondage so you can create and live the big vision you have for your personal life.

"Your Big Vision beyond the J.O.B" will show you how to tap into your passions, gifts, and talents to take control of your own destiny through entrepreneurship. Whether you have a business idea that you want to bring into reality, a cause that you are passionate about, or a desire to build wealth outside of your 9-to-5, this section will help you create a strategy while you hold down a full-time job/career.

This book will engage you, inspire you, empower you, and set you FREE. You will find my own personal journey weaved throughout the book to show you how it can be done. Your freedom is pages away in this book. Read, breathe, and run to the nearest exit with your strategy to live your big vision that's been waiting on you.

Now, turn the page and let's get you living a vibrant life!

Cherri Walston

"The BIG Vision Mentor"

THE ESCAPE ROUTE FOR
YOUR BIG VISION LIFE

KICKING DOWN THE
DOORWAY TO FREEDOM

"We all have the extraordinary coded within us waiting to be released." ~ Jean Houston

When I think about an escape route, I immediately see myself running through an open doorway to get to the other side of freedom. The escape and freedom I'm referring to is leaving the weight and heaviness in your life that imprisons you, suffocates you, stifles your growth, makes you unhappy about your life, shackles your dreams and vision, and keeps you from living an extraordinary life. I witnessed what it meant to escape from an unhealthy situation when my mother fled Philadelphia with two small children on a midnight train to North Carolina. My mother made a tough decision to leave my father for her sanity with a vision for a better life. Coming from a middle-class upbringing and having to end up living in subsidized housing (aka the projects) was unsettling for my mother. She insisted that it was a temporary situation and to not get too comfortable with our circumstances; intuitively, she knew that there was a greater plan for her life. Life seemed okay for a while until it was made known that I was different, especially immigrating from the North to the South. Different in the way I spoke—I had a Northern accent and my mother always made sure that I used the correct grammar. She would even correct my friends which was sometimes embarrassing. I was afraid they would think that I was trying to be uppity. And too, I hated the way she dressed me because I didn't look like the other kids. Sometimes she made our clothes, *and she didn't buy the fad kind of clothes*. I looked more pressed and polished so to speak. My teachers appreciated it and on every progress report they made comments about how nice and neat my mother sent me to school.

However, I never really seemed to fit in with the other girls in my community. I didn't feel smart. I was shy and I was teased a lot. I struggled to be accepted and liked, and looking back, this situation was preparing me to learn how to imagine a new reality. Just writing about this brings back some emotions of those early days. The door I was looking out of was painted with questions about my existence and why the world seemed so unkind. I was desperately seeking a way out of my own pain. I struggled to free myself from the bullies and the fiery darts of negativity that were swirling around my head. My bullies were the known bad girls in the neighborhood who would push me around, block my entrance to a path home, and threaten to beat me up and take any money I may have had on me. I'd make an excuse to be sick at times because I didn't want to go to school and have to face them; this was my only escape at the time.

My mother had an extraordinary gift for making a teepee look like a mini mansion. Although we lived in the projects, if you stepped inside our home, you would have thought we were middle-class folks. My mother was a gifted drapery-maker and a self-taught interior decorator. One of the fondest memories I have is going to work with my mother. Sometimes she didn't have a sitter for us if we were sick or out of school. She worked for a well-known decorating company in Greensboro. Back then, the company had what they called showrooms which looked like you were walking into a completely finished home. My brother and I would quietly escape downstairs to those areas and run to make our claim on one of those rooms stating, *"This is my house."* I didn't know then, but I was proclaiming—on a deeper and cellular level—a greater vision for my life. I was imaging how I wanted to live.

Meanwhile, my mother was already walking through the doorway of her escape from *project nation* when she announced that we were "finally moving" into our new home. We escaped the labeling, the stigma, and the mentality that if you lived in the projects, you would become a product of the environment. *So untrue.* To this day, no one believes that I lived in that environment for nearly nine years. It really wasn't that bad in my opinion. I never had to dodge bullets and was never approached by drug dealers. There were good families and awesome single mothers who looked after everyone's kids. I understood what it meant in that it takes a village to raise kids because back then those mothers were leading by example.

Interestingly, I wasn't quite ecstatic to leave the environment that initially made me feel less than acceptable. I had adjusted to my situation. My pathway to freedom had already opened up as I began the practicing of imagining my ideal life. If my mother could escape an unhealthy marriage of emotional stress and anxiety, a life of welfare and subsidized housing to independence from government assistance and into homeownership again, then it must really be something to this phenomena called having a vision. Our escape from *project nation* gave me a different perspective in my teens. I'd dragged those same feelings of unacceptance and wanting to fit in to a snobbish and cliquish community. I knew I was in the freedom zone, but I had some inner work to complete. I quickly resorted back to using my imagination for my ideal situation; it helped me picture what I wanted in the future. It was more of an *I'll show them* kind of thing. My journey went from childhood imagination to adulthood visualization as I learned the difference between thought and actualization. As a child, I was creating the images for what I wanted by putting thought energy into form. I probably was daydreaming—my mother not even realizing that she was showing me how to move from an idea or thought to actually projecting thought into reality. The latter is intent on a specific goal. *Bingo! Vision is the ticket to freedom, the doorway to my dream life and the escape to a new reality.*

➔ THE POWER OF VISION

I've always had a vivid imagination about how I wanted to live. It serves me well during difficult times and in setting personal goals. A vision is an internal motivator for what you aspire to have, be or do at an appointed time. A vision is where you spend quality time writing and answering questions like,

"What do I want to create for my life?" and "If I had no fear in my life, what would I be doing?" and "What do I want to contribute to my life and into others?" This process was very powerful for me and was the catalyst for my career and business launch. Having a vision gives me a sense of direction. Without it, I would flounder meaninglessly through life. A clear and vibrant vision— one that excited and propelled me to take action—sustained me during the challenging times in my life.

Proverbs 29:18 affirms that "Where there is no vision, the people will perish." Not having a vision is like having a spiritual deficiency of hope, faith and joy for what is to come. Moreover, I believe it is a GPS: God's Promise Seal on your life because you were born with greatness; it is your birthright. I've found, for the most part, that people who allow circumstances and situations to control their life don't have an internal motivator to push them forward. Even when I encountered setbacks, my vision reminded me to keep pushing. My vision for my life was plagued with doubt, fear, lack of confidence, and some perceived limitations due to the changes in my eyesight. After being diagnosed with multiple eye diseases and losing some of my peripheral vision, I wasn't sure how I would make my vision happen. I imagined being totally blind and questioned how that would impact my life. I kept my pain, struggle and diagnosis a secret and made it my personal struggle to be independent.

One day, I decided to do some research on Helen Keller. I love her quotes, especially the one that states "The best and most beautiful things in the world cannot be seen or even touched – they must be felt with the heart." As I read about her struggle and how she overcame her disability of being blind and deaf, I was inspired. Although I only had a slight impairment, I could still live my life in an extraordinary way. I realized I would have to be creative in living my dream life. I began building muscle to kick down the doorway to my freedom with an inner vision that would overpower my outer circumstance.

→ INNER VISION

I believe in living life from the inside out, being guided by your soul's calling for something greater. Herein lay the basis for seeing your future self beyond what you see with the naked eye. Your inner vision is the natural, flowing energy of how you would like to experience life. It is like having a dress rehearsal for your life and you are the star; you see yourself in every detail. Your inner vision is the most powerful gift you can have. It's so powerful that if you tap into it, there is nothing that you cannot achieve. We all were born with this inner vision. As children we created imaginary friends: little boys imagined themselves as superheroes and little girls imagined themselves as princesses. We were daring and saw possibilities that were untainted with life's uncertainties.

→ OUTER VISION

I define outer vision circumstances to be any life event, issue, self-sabotaging habit, behavior, or mindset that hinders you from living the life you were designed to live. If you don't have access to your inner light (for what you desire for your life), then you'll be tossed by every little wind that comes against you. If you want a vibrant life, then you must kick down the door that keeps you imprisoned. A vibrant life is one that makes you glow on a cellular level and feel free to pursue your dream without any limits. When you nurture your inner vision, it will keep you on course. I'm not telling you something I read, but what I know from experience. When I made the choice to be guided by the inner vision light, I stopped focusing on my perceived limitations, and, instead, focused on what I could create with what I had in front of me (limitless possibilities). Freedom was letting go of what I had gradually loss of my peripheral and 20/20 vision (my outer vision circumstance) and swinging open the doorway to a new way of looking through my heart (my inner vision light). This is where the real work begins: learning how to live from the inside out. It's possible!

→ **MANIFEST WHAT YOU WANT**

We all perceive the world differently. A person who feels like a victim of circumstances may view the world as tough and unfair. A wealthy person may view the world as a lovely place full of luxury and pleasure. Both are viewing the same world; it is just different because of their perceptions of it and their life experiences. This is true when you want to manifest a different lifestyle, a successful career, a better relationship, and so on. Sometimes it is difficult to see beyond your current reality. The key to manifestation is to make clear or evident to the inner eye (inner vision) what you desire to project into reality. That means you've got to see it first! Create what I call your "mind movie" for what you want to project into your new reality. Believe in what you want to manifest and listen to your inner voice. Manifesting is not just limited to material items. You can manifest more love, happiness, peace, etc. You can be a co-creator with God to create the world you want to live in by changing your perceptions of it, which will change your inner world.

Kicking down the doorway to freedom is an inside job with a co-conspirator, who is your inner vision. It's YOUR best plan for an EXIT strategy!

➔ **WHAT YOU'LL NEED TO ESCAPE:**

- Desire to be FREE!

- Be willing to let go of what you've lost.

- Adopt a new vision for your future self.

- Trust in your inner vision and don't be deceived by your outer vision circumstances.

- Be open to the new adventure on the other side of the door.

FREEDOM NUGGET

When you decide to escape to a new and improved life, you need to have a freedom map called **INNER VISION**.

HELP ME! I'M TRAPPED
IN MY OWN MIND

"A man will be imprisoned in a room with a door that's unlocked and opens inwards; as long as it does not occur to him to pull rather than push."— Ludwig Wittgenstein

I've coached and talked with many women, and too often I hear the clanging of chains dragging through the corridors in their mind. They speak as if they are in a holding cell. No wonder it seems too difficult to create and manifest a vision for a better life. I recently had a session with a corporate client who consistently and unconsciously closed the door by making assumptions about her opportunities before she even opened the door to possibilities. The power of the mind can free you or it can chain you. I've had to learn how to unlock the door to mind-trapping thoughts for why I couldn't pursue my vision and dreams because of my visual impairment. I was sure I was doomed, believing I was damaged and would be left alone. Who would want to be in a relationship with me?

Even more, I believed I couldn't write a paragraph that made sense, yet I completed graduate school and here I am writing my first book. This mind trap came from my junior high years of being in remedial reading classes and my college professor belittling me over an essay I wrote. He marked it up so badly that it looked blood-splattered. I was mortified! He told me I needed to go back and enroll in a composition class. I left his office and cried. At that time, I was a non-traditional student, working and going to school at night. I was tracking my credits and my money, too. I drove away, drying my tears and said, *"The hell with this. I'm not taking another class that's going to set me back."* I went to the bookstore and purchased a book on English grammar, style and writing. The funny part is, I had to take another class that was required for me to graduate and guess who was the professor? *Dang!* I was ready for him that go-round. I got an A in the class and he wrote nice comments on my papers in *black*.

Still, the encounter nearly kept me from pursuing any career opportunity that required any kind of writing. I'd immediately shy away from the word "write." What a waste of head space and stagnant energy we can emit into the atmosphere when we give power to the things we conjure up and the handcuffs we allow others to place on us. I've heard many speakers and preachers say that the mind is a battlefield; you may be feeling like you are in a war zone being held as a POW (prisoner of words). A vision can overpower the guards of your mind. That's why in Chapter One, I talked about creating a vision for your life. I see the vision as a weapon of master destruction, blasting mind traps. I'm blasting them to write this book you are reading right NOW!

→ TAKE YOUR PLACE AS CHAIRWOMAN

As a working woman, I know you've been in some non-productive meetings before. And maybe you have been on committees, boards and teams where collaborative decisions needed to be made. Some of these meetings have been unproductive, unorganized, and—need I say—unnecessary and time consuming. I am annoyed going to meetings that have no structure and are free-for-all socializing events. It's usually the meetings in which I have no investment or interest in and find myself in total oblivion as to what the heck they are talking about. It's obvious I don't like wasting my time. I can recall attending a meeting in one organization where there would be heated remarks going back and forth with comments and language that would make you cringe in disbelief. Worst of all, the chair of the meeting allowed this type of behavior to control the flow. Unwarranted, negative, nasty, and belittling comments were being hurled across the table. "Who's running this meeting?" I would ask myself. Consequently, the chair of the meeting would lose control and surrender authority to what I call "ranting committee members"—members who, at the end of the day, have no final say.

Sadly, the most powerful person in the meeting, the chair, never understood his critical role of making the ultimate decision. We contend with the same "ranting committee members" in our own lives. Ever wonder why you sabotage your success? You've given yourself so many reasons, or shall I say "excuses," why you aren't qualified, ready or deserving enough to have what you desire in your life. These "ranting committee members" reside beneath that mysterious cortex called your MIND. They are the self-talks you unconsciously give yourself when you get cold feet about writing that book, seizing an opportunity that will create a better life, following your purpose and dream, going back to school, or starting a new career or business. You name it, there's a ranting committee member hurling false predictions, lies and insults in the meeting room of your mind.

Do any of these ranting committee members sound remotely familiar to you?

- You're not a good writer. What qualifies you to even think about writing a book?

- You've taken the classes, you got the certification or have the experience, but you still don't have enough (fill in the blank).

- You tried that two years ago and it will probably fail again.

- Your (parent/teacher/friend...) said you're not good at (fill in the blank).

- If you try (fill in the blank), you might look foolish, stupid or crazy.

- You need to be like (name the person). She really has it together.

Guess what? This is the wrong time to lose control. This is your life and you are the chairwoman! A chairwoman is a woman who is the presiding officer of something such as a committee, board or meeting. That means you are officially in charge of your own mind. No longer do you need to succumb to hostile takeovers. You set the ground rules and give clear direction to make way for a productive meeting in your mind. When you have a ranting committee member who wants to shut down growth, creativity and movement with negative thoughts of why you shouldn't, couldn't and can't, lovely embrace them. Acknowledge them with gentleness. Smile and say, "I thank you for your thoughts. I never considered that. However, I have made a decision to do what is right and true for me today!" Then proceed with a plan of unwavering action. Remember, you always have the final say. It's your choice and your boardroom.

➜ GET OVER YOUR EXCUSES

I heard a multimillionaire describe excuses as well-planned lies; we tell ourselves why we can't take action on improving our current situation. If anyone knows me well, has been a client, or have had a conversation with me, I've asked them what their vision is for their lives. Sometimes I hear crickets or *"I don't know what I want to do because..."* And an excuse usually follows. Moreover, with some, it's the same excuse year after year. This is a mind-numbing effect that arrests any possibility to achieve the greatness that is within you. Excuses are a way out, a holding cell for a confined life, but not the doorway to freedom. As a coach and mentor for aspiring entrepreneurial women, I've seen two types of thinkers: The I-can't-do-that-because thinkers and the let-me-figure-out-how thinkers. The latter are grounded in belief, optimism and determination. They recognize they have some limitations, yet, they know there are other options, alternatives and behavior changes that will support what they want to do. You can come up with all kinds of reasons why something can't be done. Some may be very legitimate. However, a lot of them are well-planned lies that maybe you or someone else crafted as to why it can't happen.

Nearly twenty years ago, I was told that I would be blind. I had already planned my demise. I saw no reason to pursue my dreams, go back to school, start a business, or have a successful relationship because of my limitation. I had conjured up every possible reason and excuse why I couldn't. Thank God **faith** and **fight** kicked in in my darkest hour. I recovered and adopted the mental attitude of *let me figure out how I can do this*. Instead of excuses, I now seek solutions and alternative ways to ensure success in what I want for my life. My limitations have now become my motivation. I have achieved all the things I thought weren't possible for me. It has become a welcomed challenge for me to move beyond my perceived limitations.

Excuses have become a major mind trap for many and most people have this trouble in more than one area of their lives. As a Training & Development Professional and Visionary Entrepreneur, I've witnessed many people travel in the why-they-can't lane and never yield to move into the lane of strategies, solutions and options. What lies ahead is a mind wreck in the making with all lanes closed to happiness, joy, peace, fulfillment, contentment, and a vibrant life.

Here are some of the most common excuses:

- *I don't have the money.*

- *I don't have any time.*

- *I tried that before and it didn't work.*

- *I'm a single mom.*

- *I don't have the support I need from my husband or significant other.*

- *I'm too tired, I don't have any energy.*

- *I don't have the right...*

- *That's not for me.*

- *I need to wait until the kids...*

- *I wasn't taught how to...*

- *I didn't grow up with...*

Most of these excuses are based on fear, unbelief, and a lack of knowledge, commitment and discipline. It's too easy to talk about what you want, but it can be a little uncomfortable and risky to take the leap to make real incremental changes in your life. With a little focus and discipline, you can begin to eliminate the excuses and start examining what you can and need to let go of. There is always a way around your perceived limitations. When you get in the habit of working with what you have in front of you instead of what you can't do, your mind will be free to explore your options. STOP hiding behind your well-planned lies and examine your priorities. You will be *amazed* at what you can achieve! Be committed and open to embracing new ways and rid yourself of old habits that keep you fenced in.

➜ A PRISONER OF THE PAST AND CURRENT

Sometimes, we become prisoners of our thoughts and our past mistakes. This makes you feel underserving and unworthy for any goodness to flow into your life. Regrets block the doorway for any hope of what could be waiting for you. If only you would grab the knob and take a peek at what's waiting for you on the other side. However, as a prisoner of the past, you can do nothing. Unlike real prisoners, who are held for a specific time, you can change your circumstances at any time. What you really need is some inspiration to release the door to see a better view for your future self. Inspiration, as it is commonly understood, means to experience a state of mind that propels you to work happily, try to achieve goals, and feel good about yourself and the world. When you are not inspired and can't seem to set any goals, you feel that you are so helpless that nothing can be done.

The first thing I'd recommend is to find stories of people such as Helen Keller and other women who've overcome many difficulties to emerge victorious. Keller was my inspiration when I was a prisoner of my thoughts regarding my loss of eyesight. That will give you hope that things are not that bad. These stories will show you that your past or present circumstances does not have to be a trap but rather an opportunity to learn how to navigate a new way of being. Go back to a memory when you felt good because of something you achieved. It could be something very small, anything—buying your first car or home, landing a job on the first interview, achieving your weight goal, learning to overcome speaking in public without losing oxygen to your brain (That's me!). This will break open another door.

Now begin giving thanks for your all blessings, then and now. Do you have a functioning brain? Can you see? Can you hear? Can you smell? Can you touch? Will you sell your eyes for any price? No! Who said that you have no money? You are a wealthy person who is unaware of your wealth, your blessings. Gratitude will open one more door from captivity. Break the last door open by thinking of the goals you might want to achieve. Believe that you can do it: Start planning and think of ways you can achieve them. Be ready for a long struggle, knowing that with a firm resolve you will succeed. This will take you out of the prison of your thinking and make you a new person, ready to fight. You are already free and you don't even know it!

Here's my Six Steps to Escape the Mind Trap Formula:

1. Imagine your excuses sounding like a scratched CD. The first thing you do is STOP playing it!

2. Find a new frame of reference for why you *can* do something. It sets you up to see the various possibilities.

3. Retire the mind-numbing literature, reality TV, and people who have a jail mentality (can't see their own way out) for a 30 days and see how much better you feel.

4. Pick up an inspiring book and read it through its entirety.

5. When the negative chatter creeps in your mind, get real with her by asking, *"Who do you think you are talking to? You must not know who I am today!"*

6. Love your past and present. It's the doorway to cultivate a BIG vision.

Being aware of your barriers helps you get out of your own way and move from the *trap* to the *track* that will lead you to your destination.

FREEDOM NUGGET

You know you are free when you defy the mind a space to roam freely without questioning its erratic moves.

FEAR LOCKS,
COURAGE RELEASES

"Courage is resistance to fear, mastery of fear, not absence of fear". ~ Mark Twain

What keeps many people from moving beyond their circumstances is being locked by fear. It is usually the fear of the unknown or the *what ifs* that keep you trapped in the very place you don't want to be. Fear can cloud your thinking and your decisions and leave you ill-equipped to take the necessary action to move the stones that are blocking your path. Fear is debilitating because it robs your energy, joy and peace, and holds you back from stepping out on faith. I nearly missed out on my calling in life. I always feared speaking in front of a group, but I knew I had to overcome that fear because my goal was to pursue a career in training and development. The thought of speaking in front of people made me feel nauseated, anxious, and sometimes I felt like I was losing oxygen to my brain. I knew I could not be successful as a speaker and trainer if I continued to let fear paralyze me. So I took action and enrolled myself in a speaking club called Toastmasters where you learn the basics of public speaking and how to overcome your fear of speaking.

That was the best *fear-busting* move I could have put in place for myself. It gave me the confidence and courage I needed to believe in myself and my ability to overcome my fear of public speaking. Now I'm not saying I don't get nervous at times, but I have learned how to not let that stop me. We make ourselves crazy when all we do is think about what scares us. The more you focus on and talk about what you fear, the more it becomes a reality for you. Get to know people who are doing the things you want to do. You will be surprised that they have some of the same fears you have, but the difference is they felt the fear and did it anyway. You may not always feel comfortable or competent, but taking the first step builds courage. One thing that has always supported me was my big vision for what I really wanted to achieve. I can't stress enough how vital it is to be guided by your inner vision. That internal motivator is there to give you a gentle nudge and say, *"Go ahead, my darling. It's okay, it's what we both want."*

What are you afraid of? What's the worst that could happen? Compare the worst-case scenario as it relates to your fear to a concrete way that you know things actually are. This will help you rediscover reality. The more you can concentrate on what you know and the way things actually are, the more you will be able to focus and think about reality. Don't allow yourself to get stuck to the point where you cannot function. Incorporate a spiritual practice that you can do on a regular basis to help you through this process. I meditate and use creative visualization techniques to guide me into seeing myself in the space I desire to be. First, I set the goal or intention I desire, then I create the "mind movie" effect that I mentioned in Chapter One; I see myself actually doing the thing I fear and focus on it throughout the day or however long I need to. I also make a strong affirmative statement: *"Girl, you got this. You've been dreaming about it for a long time. Let's step into it."*

Do it in a way that your fear doesn't over-power your inner vision. Move yourself from fear to faith. If you do not have faith, you will doubt; if you doubt, you will fear; and if you fear, you will mentally relate yourself to that which you fear. If you want to be able to open the doorway for what you want, then your thoughts must be conceived in faith. Thoughts without faith have no form or creative energy. If you do not have faith in what you believe can happen, then it is really a waste of time thinking about. Moreover, you must commit to faith with action. Not doing anything will not eliminate the fear. Moving from a place of comfort will help you begin the journey of walking by faith—where you will feel the fear and act anyway. Step out with your head held up, your chest out, and your steps high. Refuse to consider yourself as anything less than a confident, competent and *courageous* woman.

Who Can Find a Courageous Woman?

Courage is not the absence of fear, but rather the judgment that something else is more important than fear.
~ Ambrose Redmoon

The brave may not live forever, but the cautious don't live at all.
~ Ashley L.

When I read Ambrose Redmoon's quote, I think about Harriet Tubman who risked being captured and killed, yet she felt it was more important to help more than 300 slaves to freedom. The second quote makes me think about every woman who has an unfulfilled dream because she drives every day, month or year riding her BRAKES. Is this you? What if you could drive everyday with anti-lock brakes in every area of your life? What would you achieve? What in your life could use more acceleration? Imagine easing off the brake pedal a little and cruising down Freedom Lane. What do you see? A confident woman taking charge of your life, writing that book you've been dreaming about, getting that degree/certification you've been putting off, releasing yourself from that job that's sucking the life out of you. Whatever you see, you must drive down Courage Lane to get there! I love how Thomas Fuller's quote describes it, *"Courage is fear holding on a minute longer."*

Who is a courageous woman? Or better yet, what does she look like?

- A single-parent raising children with little or no support.

- A woman who has been victimized but chooses not to play the victim any longer and stands up for her rights.

- A woman who is facing a life-threatening diagnosis but chooses to fight for her life.

- A woman who chooses not to stay in an unhealthy relationship because of money, status or social pressure.

- A woman who can say no and not feel guilty because she is saying YES to something greater.

- A woman who "shows up" in her life and does what she needs to do to make it happen without making excuses.

- A six-figure earning woman who decides to leave her corporate job to pursue her passion.

She is the everyday woman, like you and me, who has faced or is facing her fears head on. You have the capacity to be a courageous woman. It's your choice to access what's already inside of you. Again, it's learning to live from the inside out—being guided by your inner vision light. Having courage does not mean you have to be brave or fearless; it means seeing the *big vision* with a different frame of reference. It's a sheer act of determination to do the thing you think you cannot do. Courage also reminds me of a tree that represents strength in every season it encounters. It stands tall and continues to thrive at its best in the face of storms.

Here are four vascular walls you can build like a tree to be rooted in courage:

- **Perseverance** - During the cold winter, you may often feel lonely and question the reason for the change. You may even tremble with anxiety. Call on the power within a small, yet steady, voice that says, *"You can make it,"* and continue on with steadfast action.

- **Self-determination** – There will be days when you feel brittle as though you are breaking and your roots are paralyzed in the earth and unable to bend. Resolve to stand strong and not allow any external forces shake you. The heavens always send a warm ray of sunlight to remind you that you are not alone.

- **Confidence** – See yourself standing tall even when the leaves are falling, when the ice is forming, and as the buds are in bloom. You have the capability to thrive. Just believe in yourself.

- **Hope** – Fill your heart with the desire of what you want and expect it to happen. Someone is waiting for the fruit of your season. When winter is over, you will be overcome with joy in the realizations that you have thrived. From the vantage point of the summer, you can stand at the doorway to your vision with wonder how you made it through.

→ LIVING COURAGEOUSLY

Going after your dreams and living your vision takes a lot of discipline, focus and determination. But most of all, it takes courage—the courage to face your fears head on, to stand up to the critics, and disbelievers who threaten to sap your strength. Living your vision means living courageously, playing a bigger game and refusing to let anything get in your way, no matter how scary the path may seem. Living courageously every day is the key to creating the career, business and life of your dreams. And it starts by taking a good, hard look at what's keeping you from living your greatness. Your life is meant to be lived, not tucked away in a box collecting dust. Don't let fear of failure or the unfamiliar keep you from taking a risk. Being vulnerable is living; it opens you up to experiences you've never had.

Several years ago, I had to learn how to spread my courageous wings and emerge from a scared, insecure duckling into a soaring swan. I was finally going to pursue my passion of helping people realize their potential. After deciding to attend graduate school, I was terminated from my job. I can recall packing up my desk and taking my belongings to my car. As I sat in the parking lot, I wondered how I would pay my mortgage, my new car and tuition. As if that weren't enough, I faced losing my sight and needed immediate surgery on my eye. I didn't have health coverage. The fear of uncertainty nearly plunged me into the sea of despair. But even in the midst of uncertainty, I continuously thought about my big vision for my life which, at that time was to get my degree and work in my desired field. That day, I decided to turn fear into a fight for what I believed was my greater purpose. I rode the waves out that year and the blessings unfolded: I finished grad school, attained a job in my field, paid bills without any major losses, and didn't lose complete sight in my eye. *Whew!* That was enough to give a girl a nervous breakdown. When you have a compelling vision for your life, sometimes you'll need to take a courageous leap of faith, and not a fear limping walk, into your destiny.

You will always feel fear, especially when you are pursuing something greater than your perceived limited capacity. Let your vision be bigger than your fear. The new job will come out of the blue and the mortgage will get paid, the right person will show up, opportunities will present themselves and you will be carried through. You have one life to live, one chance and one moment at a time to create the life you want to live. Jump in with all you got and who you are.

Here are a few questions to answer as you prepare for your COURAGEOUS leap

1. What about your professional life? When it comes to what you want to achieve in your work or career, what big, scary possibilities come to mind?

2. What ideas are so powerful, so courageous that they make your heart race and your stomach a little queasy just to imagine saying yes to them?

3. Professionally and personally, where could your path of greatest courage lead? How does that path compare to the path you're currently following?

4. What is standing in the way of you following your path of greatest courage?

FREEDOM NUGGET

If you want better, challenge yourself to be better. Waiting for it won't do a thing, but **COURAGEOUS ACTION** will do the thing.

PUSH THROUGH THE OBSTACLES

"Stand up to your obstacles and do something about them. You will find that they haven't half the strength you think they have" ~ Norman Vincent Peale

Life events can sometimes impede your progress and make you question whether you should continue the journey you are on to make your goals, dreams and visions a reality. It can get tough, and at times tough enough to either cause you to readjust your sail or give up and forget you ever had a dream. I've seen many people abandon their goals because of a bump in the road that felt like a sinkhole to them. Obstacles can feel like an obstruction to your progress, but they don't mean STOP. I believe they are experiential learning opportunities, a test to your faith, character building and a way to live courageously. I have had more obstacles than

I would like to count; I'm beginning to feel like an obstacle warrior. As I look back over the years, I realize that my obstacles have given me a real reason to push harder. I'm so doggone determined to not be defeated by life's events, but to fuel my big vision for life instead. I firmly believe that obstacles show you who you are either a *champion* or a *chimp*. I have chosen to stay in the ring a little longer waiting to win my rightful title in the game of life. As I write this chapter, I am struggling with my eyesight. I'm writing with a large font, hunched over the computer with blurred vision. I was informed by my ophthalmologist that I need to see a corneal specialist and that there's a possibility that I may need a corneal transplant. This happened right before I made the decision to pursue one of my big vision goals which was to write this book. In the first chapter, I talk about having an inner vision so you can live from the inside out and not be guided by your outer vision circumstances. *Hello!* My inner vision is blaring so bright that I need shades to block the rays! I won't be controlled by this outer vision circumstance. I have work to do and I'm about purpose. I do what I CAN and leave the rest to God. Life doesn't have to be hard. You just have to be strong and determined, and I guarantee things will line up in your favor.

➜ THE OLYMPIAN EFFECT

When there is something *big* that you want to accomplish, the greater the opposition you will have to face. A great example of this is the Olympics. The athletes overcome incredible odds to be selected for the competition. They dare to dream and push themselves beyond their obstacles. Although they may miss the gold by a fraction of a second...giving up is not an option. They continue by honing their athletic ability and opening their mind to new possibilities for the gold medal. That's what you have to do. The obstacle is there to ignite the power that's within you and to offer a new way of doing things. Sometimes you can be your own obstacle. You must change your attitude about yourself and the situation you find yourself in. Olympians are always pushing themselves to new heights; as a result, they come out a better person than they were before.

→ BECOME AN OLYMPIAN

First, you must begin with the end in mind. Think about the results you want and how it feels to be on the other side of victory; it will give you the fuel you need to propel you forward. Second, you must show up ready for the challenge. Olympians are focused and devoted to the training that is required of them. Even when they face an obstacle like injuries, they don't stay down, they get back in the game.

Disappointments will happen and feeling defeated will cause you to lose your footing and make it hard for you to climb back up. Keep running and let the wind of determination keep you on track. There is an Olympian in YOU, waiting to be lifted to new heights. You can't just throw in the towel because something didn't work the first, second, or third time. You have got to fail forward! Olympians aren't made overnight.

If you remember watching the 2008 Olympics, 41-year-old Dara Torres was the first American swimmer to compete in five Olympics and was the oldest to qualify for the games. Dara won several medals, retired in 1992, and for the next seven years, she married, divorced, did broadcasting for a Golf Channel, and had a baby. She resumed training for two years to qualify for the 2008 games. She ended up missing four weeks of training to repair a rotator cuff tear in her right shoulder, but didn't skip a beat at the Olympic trials. The media repeatedly harped on the fact that she was the oldest swimmer. I love her response: *"The water doesn't know how old you are."*

Winners understand the power of discipline. You cannot get what you never had unless you are willing to do what you have never done. You can train your body to be an Olympian. However, the difference in winning or losing is not going to be training the body, it's going to be training your mind to think positive. It's those powerful thoughts that believe you can do it. Olympians are committed to their goals. They know firsthand that it may take years to compete and qualify, but giving up is not an option for them; their eye is on achieving an excellent start and finish. Sure they have setbacks, heartaches and disappointments, but they understand that that's what it takes to compete. They're not focused on what they will have to give up, but what they will gain in the process. It is a journey and like most journeys, they can be paved with obstacles. Olympians know the cost and the valuable lessons that come along with them. Success isn't about winning. It's saying, yes, I went all the way, in spite of.

➜ FAILURE IS NOT AN OBSTACLE

The biggest obstacle to success for most people is the fear of failing. Failure is only a negative event when you allow it to become an obstacle to your success. I quickly grasped the concept of failure when I decided to explore a new and different approach in my business. My first attempt bombed!

The second attempt was slightly better, but I still didn't get the results I was hoping for. These attempts, along with constant tweaks in the process, showed me a new way of looking at failing that I'd never considered in my past failures.

Here's what I discovered in the process:

- Failing is a natural process for me to simply collect the data/knowledge that I needed to try it again.

- The quality and quantity of that data/knowledge was tied to my success.

- The faster I was willing to accumulate the data/knowledge, the quicker I was able to weed out dead ends and create the results I was looking for.

- The fastest way for me to increase my success cycle was to eliminate the fear by assessing my mistakes and implementing a new action.

The more you fail, the faster you learn and grow. The word failure conjures up negative energy, concepts and images for some people. Let's say you tried something and the results weren't favorable. Now you are ready to surrender. Instead of giving up, use the opportunity to evaluate the experience. You can step back to observe, tweak, plan, and take action again. This is the easiest way to look fear straight in the eyes; that's what it takes to increase your success rate. We also have to be aware of how our ego might be feeding our fear of failure. Is your fear of failure tied to your status, finances or position? Are you more concerned with what others might think? Life itself is failure based. We wouldn't be where we are and who we are if it wasn't for our own experiences and those of our ancestors. So fail forward...for it's the quickest way to shorten your path to success.

→ SEEING THE OBSTACLE WITH A DIFFERENT LENS

Sometimes the outer vision circumstances you encounter may appear larger than life and cause you to become paralyzed in your ability to see and think clearly. Every person in their lifetime will be confronted with a mountain experience where it feels as though you can't climb it, cross it or survive the blizzard-like conditions. Nonetheless, at these seemingly bleak times, you can find the courage to face the obstacle with steadfast determination to chip away one stone at a time. You can't get a glimpse of the top of the mountain until you begin to move small stones, then you will see how low it really was. Looking at your obstacle through new lens can be a slow, yet, achievable plight. In her book, *Courage: The Heart and Soul of Every Woman*, Sandra Ford Walston writes:

> *"Vision is how you see yourself and your choices in life. Is your life filled with courage and choices, or is it one mired in a repetition of mistakes? Self-deception can be a problem when you try to create your vision. Blindness is not a virtue! Yet your vision must be designed by your heart, not your eyes."*

Changing your lens on how you see your obstacles means simply looking at yourself and the mountain you are encountering with new eyes. Do you see yourself as helpless? Or do you see yourself as an overcomer? What are you saying to yourself? I keep making the same mistakes over and over,

I'm not smart enough, I can't see myself doing that, or I don't see my situation getting any better. How tempting it is to just crawl under a rock and wait to be crushed? You leave no space for your circumstances to change by planting weeds instead of seeds. Every time you look through the window of your life, all you'll see is frustration and disappointment. You can start changing how you see your situation today.

Here are things you can start doing:

- Accept your current reality...It is what it is.

- Stop focusing so much on the negative aspect of your situation. The more you do, the more you become drained and depressed.

- Speak power to yourself/situation. For example, *"I am coming out of this situation a stronger and a wiser person."*

- Be grateful every day for what you have, not what you don't have.

- Stop living in regret and work toward what you can change in the present.

It is so easy to get caught up in regrets, disappointments, anger and feelings of despair. I am not saying that you shouldn't feel this way. There are times when you must grieve through a process. However, don't allow yourself to get emotionally handcuffed in this mode. Changing your lens may simply mean you may have to remove yourself from the situation if that is an option. In addition, your thoughts have a way of shaping your actions and feelings. What are you thinking about most of the time? What are you saying to yourself? Are you constantly worrying? Sitting around and thinking about what isn't working will not move you forward. Shift your thoughts to new ways of thinking like: *What can I do differently that I haven't tried before? How can I create the circumstances I want and not be controlled by my circumstances?*

Look at your obstacles with new eyes, seeing possibilities, opportunities and personal growth. Your situation may not change right away, but you can change how you view it. Negatively or positively, the choice is yours. I guarantee that a better outlook will keep the stones from piling up and make it easier to move forward. Change your lens so you can begin to see the light at the doorway to freedom.

→ GEAR UP FOR THE PUSH

Be prepared for oppositions that may show up as disapproval from family members and friends, or any distraction that tries to throw you off track from pursuing your goals. See it for what it is—an obstacle that wants your attention. Embrace it with understanding and love. Every time you have to scale a mountain-sized obstacle, always carry a backpack filled with grace to sustain you in times of trouble. Moreover, having faith and belief in yourself will help keep you in position should the altitude change in your situation. Stepping out of your comfort zone will be an act of courage, especially when your situation requires you to take a different route to get to the other side of the door. Don't allow yourself to be overcome by fear. Just push one stone at a time while using a fighting spirit of perseverance, self-determination, confidence, and hope. Soon, you'll be pushing boulders.

You can move any obstacle that is hindering you from experiencing the life you want by, again, changing your view of the situation. How do you see yourself? Do you see yourself as a strong oak tree that withstands the seasons of change or a broken branch waiting to be tossed in the fire? Everything you need to leap through the doorway of freedom is inside of YOU! It is waiting for you to make the choice to change your view. Hopelessness, despair, anger, or fear will not move you to the desired state of courage. You can decide that in spite of what you feel, you have the strength, power and the sheer fortitude to transform that situation into sizable chucks and gear up for the climb. You got moxie! You just needed an opportunity to showcase it. In the next chapter, you'll learn how to eliminate the behaviors that are blocking the doorway so you can tap into your greatness for the BIGGER things you want for your life. **This is not the time to quit. Keep pushing!**

FREEDOM NUGGET

You greatest triumph is not staying down when you have fallen, but rising to greet an opportunity for victory.

5

OPEN THE DOOR TO YOUR BIG VISION

"Every exit is like an entry somewhere else." ~Tom Stoppard

May I ask you a personal question? Since I've been transparent with you about my stuff, I feel like I can talk woman-to-woman with you. It's freeing when you can be honest about yourself and where you are. That's why I really wanted to write this book. I understand what it's like to have a career or a job and still feel unfulfilled and disillusioned about living someone else's vision or dream and not your own. Here it goes:

How much more time are you going to waste talking about what you want while failing to take action to do something about it?

I had to get real with you because I want to see you live your life by design and not by circumstances. You will have to stop hiding behind the door and leave your comfort zone in order to exit from your current lifestyle and into your desired lifestyle. **So what is your big vision for your life?** Is it:

- Incorporating a healthy lifestyle to have more energy to pursue your goals?

- Starting your own business?

- Gaining a better job or promotion?

- Being more confident and courageous?

- Earning more money?

- Writing your first book?

- Living a more fulfilling and purpose-driven life?

- Living your life on your own terms?

If you want these things and more, you must create a compelling *inner vision* that will spring you out of hiding and into action to bring your big vision to life.

→ HIDING BEHAVIORS

Ever wonder why your career or entrepreneurial venture seemed to fail to launch or fail to be what you desired it to be? The real truth is your behavior. These are behaviors you may or may not be consciously aware of, but if you really dig deep enough you will discover that you haven't been much of a "seeker" in exercising your *greatness*. What you have been communicating and actually doing is playing "peek-a-boo." Instead of putting yourself out there and getting known in the workplace or the marketplace, you do a little here and a little there. Here's what hiding behaviors might look like:

- **The Perpetual Student** - "I'm almost there. I need more training, seminars, etc." The perpetual student is always preparing, never doing.

- **The Marketing/Branding Wimp** - "I'll do a little and leave the rest to chance."

- **The Scaredy Cat** - "I don't want to be in their face." The scaredy cat is afraid of appearing aggressive.

- **The Procrastinator** - "I'll do it tomorrow." The procrastinator waits until the last minute, pushing it off until next week, next month, next year...

- **The She-Who-Would-Be-Everything** - "I can do it all." This woman wants to do everything, never committing to one thing and doing it well.

→ → →

You may be hiding your greatness for many reasons— reasons that keep you on the launching pad so long that you lose your flame for what you once hoped for. So why aren't you being your greatest self?

Some of those reasons may be...

- You become big and powerful in the world.

- You might fail and fear how that is going to look to your colleagues, friends and family.

- You feel like an imposter, believing that you aren't as smart as you appear to be.

- You may look or sound stupid.

- Your spouse or family members may not be supportive.

- Your success will lead you far from your comfort zone.

- You fear making powerful connections and having influence.

- You're concerned about what will people think.

- You don't feel good enough, smart enough, or pretty enough.

- You fear you won't be accepted.

- You think your vision, goal or dream is just wishful thinking.

- You're uncomfortable, embarrassed or unhappy with your financial situation.

"What is it costing you to stay hidden from living your vibrant vision?"

➜ STOP HIDING BEHIND THE DOOR

What's nudging you that you can't shake? What's keeping you lying awake at night? Are you watching everyone else live their vision while you still wait on the right time, more knowledge, more money, etc.? I am often struck by the number of women who have extraordinary gifts and talents, but are afraid to expose them to the world. Are you that woman you know who's hiding her greatness? You have something unique and special to offer. Oftentimes, you hold back and only scratch the surface of what you could be and do. You're hiding because of something in your past that you feel shame behind, an incident that you felt shut the door to a promising future, or an erroneous message that you gave too much "air-time" to. You may be in a job or career that stifles your creativity and growth, but for some unconscious reason, you have chosen to sit quietly and hope for the best. Or maybe you have this great idea for a business and you've done all the leg work to get it going but fail to launch.

Do you remember playing the game hide and seek as a child? The person hiding goes to great lengths to be inconspicuous (ducking, dodging and shifting places) to not be found. However, the seeker takes great pride in the ability to launch into action because he/she is determined to bring to light what is hidden. The seeker is on a path to greatness which leads to endless possibilities and new discoveries. Think about it: It takes more effort to hide and stay small than to come out of hiding and be *free* to live your life and take advantage of the greatness that is within you.

I get it though, I initially had a problem with "failure to launch" in the workplace before I made the transition to explore my greatness. I clung to the safe positions. You know, the ones that keep you hidden in a cubicle, never challenging your intellect, never requiring you to present an idea or project, the one that pigeonholed you. The moment I made the decision to come out of hiding and step into a professional career of helping others realize their greatness, my life changed in ways I never imagined. I was developing into a courageous woman living by divine design.

→ YOUR DNA IS POWER!

When I was able to tap into my Divine Natural Abilities (DNA), I was on the path of living my *inner vision* with focused intention. I felt vibrant and alive as I opened the door to what my soul desired—doing heart-centered work! I define DNA as:

D: Divine
  – of supreme excellence; worthy; godlike characteristics

N: Natural
  – those innate things that are a part of who you are

A: Abilities
  – skills, talents, qualities and attributes you possess

It is in your **DNA** to succeed! You were born great. You already have everything you need, want and choose to be. That is a fact! All that is required of you is to tap into this greatness every day. When you are living in alignment with your **D**ivine **N**atural **A**bilities, you are living purposely, fulfilling your assignment on this earth. This not about perfection. It is not about your material possessions, your wealth, your status, your title, your position, or your social status; it is about being authentically present. What I mean by authentic presence is walking in your own truth.

What does it mean to walk in your own truth?

- You express your gifts through dance, music, art, writing, drama, or other expressive ways.

- You show up unfazed by judgments or criticism because of others' lack of understanding.

- You don't worry with what other people think you should be doing.

- You are being and doing what is true for you today!

- You can stand out in a crowd and not feel uncomfortable about your choice of style or anything that sets you apart. You have your own personal brand.

When you are walking in your Divine Natural Abilities, you don't have to be someone else other than yourself. You don't have to make excuses about who you are. You were equipped from birth with a purpose. You were created in a God-like image; this is the origin of your DNA! You have greatness inside you even though you may not have lived fully into it, it's there for your access. The secret ingredient is inside of YOU! You have got to stir it up every day.

Here are some very important questions I want you to ponder as you think about the power of your DNA so you can ignite your inner passion and live your inner vision:

[The **DNA** Test]
Have you tested your gift? Have you uncovered your purpose or operated in your purpose? Have you tested your strength and your courage by doing something that made your knees shake? You must do something that is going to stretch you beyond your comfort level.

[The **DNA** Results]
Did you panic or shy away from what you discovered? Did you find out that you are really good at something that others can benefit from only to learn that it is going to require you to come out of hiding? Are you questioning the legitimacy of your results because you don't believe you are equipped to take full action on it?

[The **DNA** Truth About YOU]
You are beautiful, brilliant, smart, intelligent, creative, loving, kind, and thoughtful. You have business savvy, you're courageous, you're resilient, and you are great! You are MORE than enough!

Here are four steps to activate your Divine Natural Abilities (DNA):

1. Step back from everything and be the observer of your life: get clear about what you want. See how your Divine Natural Abilities can help you achieve what it is you desire and uncover the obstacles that can get in your way.

2. Take responsibility of what you have uncovered in Step 1 and begin to create the life or situation you want. Take control of your life by doing something. Don't just wait around for something to happen or continuously talk about it. If you want something bad enough then you have to do something about it. Stop complaining, stop blaming and stop playing around with the idea. You are responsible for your life. Do the necessary work to make it happen.

3. Beginning today, start living in your Divine Natural Abilities on a daily basis. Make daily choices that support your DNA. Be about business and not busyness. Having a lot going on doesn't mean you are about business and on purpose. Have a purposeful intent.

4. Walk in your Divine Natural Abilities with boldness, conviction and continue as it starts to become a way of life for YOU!

→ LIVE YOUR BIG VISION

Imagine for a moment that there was a way for you to ignite your inner vision so you could live your *big vision.* What would you be doing? If you knew there was a way to free yourself from the 9 to-5 mindset so you could bring your big vision idea, goal, or lifestyle into existence, how would you show up every day? The answer may seem somewhat hidden, but I assure you that it isn't. You can open the door to a vibrant life and bring your big vision into reality. The exit strategy is to move from moment to moment with a sense of urgency!

Have you seen in a boxing match where the boxers accidently bump heads in the ring and one gets a cut over their eye? He begins moving around the ring with a sense of urgency as if his life depends on it. Why? Because there's a lot at stake—the referee can now stop the fight at any moment. You must attack the big vison you want to bring to life each day, hour and minute with the same sense of urgency. If you never made time to write down your personal vision or never followed through on your goals to completion, now is the time to move with a sense of urgency. Ignite a sense of urgency by creating a compelling inner vision that excites, inspires and moves you with a quickness to see it through the end. When you approach your day in this way, in no time you'll begin to see a new woman staring back at you in the mirror. Living in a state of urgency tells the mind that you are going to be relentless until you meet success. Urgency provides immediate focus to the big vision you want to call forth. Before you know it, momentum builds and carries you towards achievement. Waking up at 5:30 a.m. each morning to some would be unimaginable. To me, it is my way of preparing to be the best coach, mentor and entrepreneur I envision myself to be. With a sense of urgency, you perform at a higher level of accomplishment.

You have the master key to unlock the door and exit into your desired reality. What are you waiting on? I believe you can do it. No, I *know* you can do it! Think about how fulfilling your life can be and the rewards you can receive from living your life from the inside out: walking in your true calling, a soul-connected career and or business, and a vibrant life that transcends a mediocre life. Now that you've cleared the doorway of the obstacles that were blocking your entrance to attaining your big vision, it's time to celebrate your freedom. You are no longer bonded! You can start living and not talking about the life you want. I'm excited for you because a life with vision is like sunshine on a cloudy day—your path will be illuminated no matter what!

If you want to know how to transition from Employee to an Employed-preneur (starting a business while working your full-time job), then read on to the next section of this book. You can have a big vision beyond your 9-to-5 too!

FREEDOM NUGGET

If there's anything worthwhile achieving in life, you have to push through the **PAIN** (perfection, adversity, idleness and naysayers). They all rob you of living your vision.

YOUR BIG VISION BEYOND THE J.O.B

6

CHANGING LANES:
TAKING A SCENIC ROUTE

"If you don't know where you are going, any road will get your there." ~Lewis Carroll

Have you ever been driving in the fast lane and realized you needed to slow down and change lanes? This can happen in real life situations where you come face to face with having to take a different direction in life. It's like you're driving eighty miles an hour trying to reach your destination when suddenly you run into a detour. Now you've entered a road less traveled. I experienced this very same feeling when I had to make a detour in my career after being laid off twice. It was in those transitional moments that I had to slow down and get quiet. As I began to create visual images of what I desired on the detour and how I wanted to live the rest of my life, I realized I had to travel through unknown territory that would require a BIG stretch for me. I was terrified, but the passion and desire for the vision had overtaken me. I knew I had to change lanes or risk being run over by my own fears, self-doubt and uncertainty about what lay ahead.

I see it every day. Friends, clients and family members who are in careers where they feel trapped, don't know where to turn next, or they've been thinking about starting a business but it feels too scary. Better yet, I hear: *"I better keep the job I have, it's better than not having nothing."* Sound familiar? But here's the caveat, if you are looking for a deeper sense of fulfillment, purpose and soul-connection in your job, you will not find it unless you unite who you are with what you do. Moreover, your job is not a security blanket that you can carry around and feel safe. You might have to one day make a detour and change your course of action. It's hard to embark on a new venture and even harder to let your dream and vision die because you want to believe you are safe where you are.

Find yourself and express yourself in your own unique way. Express your passion openly. Life is nothing but a dream and if you create your life with passion, your dream becomes a masterpiece of art.

➜ CREATING A NEW MASTERPIECE

I enjoy great works of art, painting, writing, architectural buildings and spaces. They are the outcome of imagination, vision and genius. Wise mentors have taught me that when you discover and use your gifts, you can create a masterpiece of your own life. Whether it's on a grand scope or a small scale, you can touch the lives of those around you. You must trust that you can create your individual masterpiece. Nothing resonates more than your own individuality. You become your own work of art when you understand who you are and express it in a unique and authentic way. In the business arena, it is known as branding.

Many times we walk around blind, unaware and unconscious of the work of art we truly are. We have been endowed with the power of choices that reside within us, yet all the tools and colors that make us originals have been handed over by others in the institutional silos we call jobs. Why not choose your own landscape, the background, the scheme of colors, the medium and your own brush strokes with consciousness and full awareness. Create your life in a way that when you stand back from the canvas and pause at it all, it is with great pride and joy in what's shaping up to be a masterpiece. Is that not the purpose of the Master who created you in the first place? What lies between where you are now and what you want to create beyond your 9- to-5 is a seed that needs to be planted in rich soil. Like an artist, you can set out to create your own masterpiece.

Here are few steps involved in creating a masterpiece for your life beyond the 9-to-5:

- **Study your Subject.** Examine who you are and what makes you unique.

- **Identify your BIG Shapes.** It may look like a puzzle in the beginning—organize and arrange your skills and strengths until shape begins to take place.

- **Underpaint your canvas.** Freely create your vision of how you see yourself. Don't worry about filling in the details yet.

- **Study your color values.** See the value of your masterpiece (YOU)—the beauty of the vision first, then work the colors (Personality, **D**ivine **N**atural **A**bility, Values) in.

- **Block in your colors.** Carefully fill in the colors of your uniqueness as you see them, leaving nothing out.

- **Adjust your color and value.** Make adjustments as you see them appear. Don't allow others to paint for you; a masterpiece is authentic.

- **Finish your painting.** Resist the temptation to finish it too soon because you may leave out some important shapes, colors and details. Step back, get out of the way as there will be more work to do.

This process requires lots of love and patience with yourself because you are changing lanes, changing landscapes and creating something magnificent where you are infusing your divine self into a masterpiece for you and the people whose life will be enriched by it.

➜ EXIT TRAPS ALONG THE WAY

The comfort zone is a dangerous place to take residence if you are looking to one day leave your job for full-time entrepreneurship, launch a business while you work, create wealth beyond your 9-to-5, and engage in soul-fulfilling work that perhaps your day job just doesn't fulfill. As good and as enticing as it is to play safe or play small, in the end you are robbed of your happiness, contentment, peace, and the joy of life. When you begin to change lanes in your professional life to pursue something that speaks to your soul's purpose beyond your job, you may run into some exit traps along the way. These traps can easily misguide you from taking the scenic route of creating your masterpiece to a dead end zone. The exit traps could look like this:

➔ TRYING TO CONVINCE OTHERS ABOUT YOUR DECISION

There is nothing more self-defeating than to make a decision and then spend endless time trying to convince other people to buy into it. I met a woman who was so excited about starting her own business of making a difference in the lives of the people she desired to serve while creating wealth for herself and family. She spoke with her family about it and decided to make an investment in the business. However, she hasn't moved beyond her investment. One day, I asked her what was going on. She replied, *"I'm still talking to my family about it."* Stand in your power of choice and believe you are capable of making a decision that is right for you.

➔ LIVING IN THE ILLUSION OF TIME

How many times have you said, *"I don't have time to do that. I have so much on my plate now."*? In reality, you are really distracted by other things in your life that you are attached to. Kim George, in her book, *Coaching into Greatness*, identifies an equation that explains why you don't have enough time to do what you *can* do: Distraction + Justification = **Avoidance**. What you are really saying is it's not that important. Most importantly, this is another excuse for procrastination or fear of failure. Safety in the illusion of time becomes convenient to stay small and not reach for the stars.

→ FOCUSING TOO MUCH ATTENTION ON THE EXTERNAL - NOT ON THE INTERNAL

Women seem to fall into this trap unconsciously. It amazes me to see women spend enormous amounts of time and money to look beautiful on the outside. Believe me, I love to look good and believe whole-heartedly in taking care of myself. Unfortunately, too many women stop there. Personal development is vital for your emotional, spiritual, intellectual and mental stability. It is an ongoing journey of self-improvement and self-discovery. If you want to make changes in your life, you must take small steps every day. Observe and pay attention to what's going on in your life. See what's getting in your way. Outer accessories are temporal, your inner spirit cries for attention. Stop, look and listen!

→ NEVER ACCEPTING GOOD ENOUGH

This is definitely a "show stopper." Being prepared doesn't have a lot to do with this one. I know many individuals who have all the credentials, accolades, accomplishments and more, yet still see themselves as not being *good enough*. I've been there myself before. The culprit is unbelief. The truth is that you already have what you need to do and be who you are. It's just waiting for you to walk in your greatness and BE IT!

➜ ALLOWING SITUATIONS AND CIRCUMSTANCES DICTATE YOUR LIFE

I love it when George Bernard Shaw said, *"People are always blaming circumstances for what they are. I do not believe in circumstances. The people who get on in this world are the people who get up and look for the circumstances they want, and if they cannot find them, they make them."* I also believe that if you shift from a "problem state of mind" to a "solution state of mind," you will find your way. There isn't anything you can't achieve when you have a vision for your life. You might have to make some adjustments or take a different route, but if you have the compass for your life (the vision), you're sure to find your way. Winners look for ways to overcome the obstacles; whiners moan, groan and focus on how painful it is to keep going.

➜ FILLING EVERYBODY'S CUP—EXCEPT YOUR OWN

"In case we lose air pressure in the cabin, the oxygen masks will drop. If you have a child, please put your mask on first, before you put on theirs." There is an obvious reason for that. You can't pour into everyone else and still have some left for yourself. There is nothing wrong with taking care of your family, serving in your faith community or sowing into the lives of others. I have heard countless stories from people who have regrets about how they invested their energy and resources into others and didn't get a chance to pursue what they wanted in life. Find a balance and set some boundaries so you won't have to look back and ask...*where did my life go?* Being aware of your own barriers can help you get out of your own way and

move from the *trap* to the *track* that will lead you to your destination.

→ BEYOND THE CUBICLE CELL

When I encountered being downsized twice in my professional career, the second time I asked, *"Where do I go from here?"* I quickly knew it was a call to action, because I'd been wrestling in my spirit for a long time about starting a business. I knew I wanted to continue to help people achieve their desired goals in life. Moreover, I was already doing this in my professional career as a trainer, but I wanted to take it to another level. I had no clue as to how I was going to change lanes and chart a new path. During one of my career transitions, I decided to devote my spare time in volunteering for a women's center in my area. That experience shifted my life in ways I would have never imagined. My dream had awakened me to a new reality that was right in front of my eyes. From there, I committed my life to helping other women move from dreaming to living the life they desired. This awakening culminated into a professional coach certification and the development of two business concepts that supported women in creating their vision and bringing it to life. Interestingly, in 1997, as I was planning my future and writing down my goals, I wrote I wanted to have a business one day. That dream is now a reality! If it happened for me, it can surely happen for YOU too.

If you have a passion for something that you want to turn into a business concept or you have been thinking about starting a business but don't know where to start, then continue reading to the next chapter as I share how to turn your passion into a business concept. You don't have to stay stuck in a dead end career, you can cultivate your entrepreneurial pursuits while you hold down a full-time job. It won't always be easy, but if you desire greater for your life, then you can start where you are and build something that's meaningful and rewarding. Don't let your job or career stifle your divine gifts and talents. Get your idea out of your head and into a plan of action. You can start preparing for your exit strategy now and determine when and how long you want to stay in Corporate America. You lead and leave on your own terms!

If you desire more freedom and flexibility in your life, then you can start by aligning your personal vision for your life from the first section in the book with your business idea or, what I like to call, your passion business. Being an Employed-preneur is a worthwhile commitment. What big vision business idea would you like to bring into reality? It's an exciting time to be a woman entrepreneur. It's even more exciting to bring forth that idea you want to express to the world and make a profit getting your message, services or products out to your ideal market.

Imagine living out that business idea you have been dreaming about for a long time now. What would that idea mean for you, your family, your community, and the people you desire to serve? The beauty of this idea is that everybody benefits from it in a special and unique way. Think about that idea not coming to fruition. *How many people won't get the help, support or service they desperately need if you don't act.*

FREEDOM NUGGET

If you are still complaining about your job, then maybe it's time to work on your own vision and **STOP** complaining about someone else's. They aren't going anywhere—it's their creation.

7

PASSION: THE FIRE ESCAPE ROUTE TO YOUR NEW ADVENTURE

"Are you bored with life? Then throw yourself into some work you believe in with all your heart, live for it, die for it, and you will find happiness that you had thought could never be yours." ~ Dale Carnegie

I read an interesting story about a woman who worked very hard in her job. She attained a college degree in an area of interest and got a job working in her chosen field. She had a loving husband and they had two wonderful children. Life was good in her adult years, but she found herself feeling like she was just on the treadmill of life. She got up every morning, went to a job that she liked but where she longed for a desired break. This woman lost most of her hobbies due to the time restraints of working many hours on the job, balanced with trying to take care of and spend time with her family. The dreams she spoke about in her youth (travel, starting her own business, becoming classical pianist, etc.) were still in the back of her mind, but only faintly. She had a successful life by American standards (income, job, home, family, etc.), but she did not leap out of bed in the morning; she did not have a spring in her step and she seemed to carry a high level of stress. In essence, she was happy, but not really HAPPY. This story may resonate with you in some or all aspects of your life as a woman with a great life, but lacking *passion*.

However, you may be on the flipside of the coin as a woman with passion but can't seem to express it in a way that reflects your vision or personality. You may feel trapped, suffocated or boxed in in your job or career. Even more, you may have passion, yet your company may not recognize or appreciate your contributions; they just want you to be robotic in your day-to-day functions. Your passion gets muted and tucked under your desk. You try to pull it out every now and then, but receive stares from your counterparts who just don't get it. Don't blame them; it's not totally their fault. It's what generally happens over time when you've been institutionalized and have to play by someone else's rules and live out their ideals. It's an on-the-job hazard! And what generally happens sometimes is people began to conform to a culture that doesn't value creativity for authenticity. This may be why you feel bored, misplaced, rejected, underutilized, uninspired, and just flat out disenchanted with your future in the workplace. It's a chore to keep passion confined. Passion requires an open doorway to roam freely! When contained, it can wreak some emotional damage: depression, anxiety, stress, unhappiness, resentment, and deprivation of joy.

Webster's Dictionary defines passion as "a strong desire for or devotion to some activity, object, or concept." Passion is not something that is obvious like being a gifted musician, singer, or a talented artist. Passion is not on the conscious level, something you are thinking about or noticing. It is more "energetic" in nature. People can confuse passion with purpose. For instance, this book embodies my purpose as my passion is to educate, inspire, encourage and empower you to live your inner vision. Purpose is what you do (i.e. writing music, parenting, and teaching). Passion is the energy you need to power up your gift, talent or skill (i.e. by creativity, problem solving or helping people). Passion is that internal burning you get inside when you are using your gifts, talents and purpose here on earth. You have passion before you use it. It is like an unlit candle waiting to be illuminated and shared with others!

"A candle loses nothing by lighting another candle."
~ James Keller

Your passion gets lit when you use your gifts, talents, purpose combined with your vision. It results in personal fulfillment and feels like you are in the "flow of life." You'll notice that everything starts to work together and everything in your life is filled with joy, contentment and synergy.

→ REIGNITE THE PASSION

Are you pursuing the things that fulfill your passion in life? Were you once passionate about an idea you wanted to pursue, but the flame kind of died? Your passion may have gotten hijacked by a myriad of things you have to juggle such as work, family and other commitments. This is why it's critical to create a vision; it's your co-pilot helping you land at your desired destination. Because life keeps going in spite of your vision and you need a navigator to steer you through the air pockets and through the altitude changes. Passion and vision are co-captains on your big vision path. When you reconnect with your passion, you will feel energized and ready to pursue your higher calling, your dream, your purpose and your big vision. I've encountered many unhappy women in the workplace who are unfulfilled in their roles and positions. One of the main reasons is because it doesn't embody their truest self or values. The good news is that you don't have to stay miserable! See your big vision beyond your 9-to-5 with a renewed inner vision as you begin to project what you want into your current reality. With focused intentions, you can arouse and ignite your passion for your new adventure.

Here are eight ways to arouse and ignite effective action into your passion:

1. **Create a mission statement.** Think about what cause, group, community or individuals could benefit from what you have to offer.

2. **Revisit your vision or create a new one for the season your life is in now.** Where do you want to be, do or have in the future?

3. **Get a passion boost.** Connect with other passionate people who have direction and are living their passion.

4. **Immerse yourself in inspiring materials.** Your mind will feed on what you put into it. Let it be good.

5. **See the possibilities.** Have faith and believe in the unseen and live as if it is so.

6. **Hear with new ears.** Flip the script on naysayers who think your passion has no wings. Say to yourself, *"My passion is a gift for me to express it in a way that will bless, empower and inspire others."*

7. **Give thanks for the abundance in your life.** A feeling of scarcity leaves no room to receive what is meant for you.

8. **Be of service to others.** Put your passion to the test. It helps you see the value in your gift.

A combination of these ideas can naturally create enthusiasm in you again. Start pursuing the things that fill you with passion today and you'll experience a different YOU. After all, it's what you're meant to do.

➜ FINDING YOUR VOICE

I attended a business conference in Nashville for women who were part of a personal development company called Compass in direct sales, providing affordable coaching services for women and teens. It felt like I was in an atmosphere filled with honey bees buzzing with excitement, exhilaration and undeniable passion that permeated the room. We shared the same passion for personal development. Like many of those women, I am passionate about empowering other women to live their greatness in every aspect of their lives. I attended this conference for the soul purpose of *firing* up my purpose and passion in a way that will take my business in a new and prosperous direction. I wanted to connect with other like-minded women who understood how valuable our services and programs were to women who want more for their lives in the areas of health and wellness, money and career, life balance, and relationships. I was in perfect harmony and had joined with this company because they understood my vision for helping women have a better quality of life. While working a full-time job as Training and Development Professional and building my own coaching business, I needed to keep my fire lit, so I could keep my inner vision light glowing. I needed to find my voice again to reconnect with my personal message. I was looking for an adventurous way to support my vision and I knew I was in the right place at the right time.

No matter where you are in life, there's always room for untapped possibilities. . .

As an aspiring entrepreneurial and professional woman, you probably have grappled with pursuing your entrepreneurial dream, balancing the care of your family, being pulled in many directions at work, and maintaining other commitments you have taken on. And now you have lost your voice. Maybe you lost your voice because your personal message is misaligned with the corporate, company or organizational message. It feels like you're tone deaf singing in the alto key but you really have a soprano voice; you're on a high frequency operating in a low frequency environment. The voice is the message you want reverberated through your purpose and passion; it's the cause you feel strongly about, the people you want to serve, and that thing you know without a doubt you are meant to do.

During the conference, I found myself reflecting on *why* I was so hungry to make this business of helping women bring their big vision to life. I realized my voice and message needed some vocal tuning. I hadn't been voicing my passion in a way that stirred me up in the past. If you want to be heard again, you must sing louder.

- If you want to sing in a higher octave, a message that speaks to your soul beyond your day job and convert that message into a profitable enterprise that supports your big vision lifestyle, then it's time to turn up the volume. Start by connecting with what ignites the fire in you. What energizes your soul when you think or talk about it?

- Think about how you can share it with others who need your message and what you have to offer.

- Embrace the fact that you have a unique voice/message that needs to be heard.

It's time to unleash your true self, your vision, your value, and your unique gifts and talents to the people who are looking for ways to improve their quality of life. Are you ready to explore how to tap into your entrepreneurial brilliance? Read on as we get you fired up to take the exit route from passion to turning your big vision idea into a profit generating business you love!

Questions to ignite and connect you with your passion business idea:

- What would be different or possible if you could express your passion using your divine gifts and talents every day?

- What is it costing you to stay silent (not being able to voice your message)?

- What are you passionate about that you could possibly see as a business opportunity?

FREEDOM NUGGET

Your light shines when you are living your passion and sharing your gifts with the world. People, clients and family will bask in your glow.

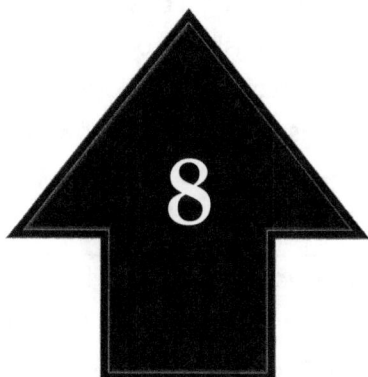

SCRATCHING THE ENTREPRENEURIAL ITCH

"The best way to predict the future is to create it."
~ Peter Drucker

D o you know the single most important choice you can make when it comes to turning your passion into a profit? The answer is simple: make sure there is a strong desire between your passion and your business idea. There is nothing else more significant than ensuring your ideal business satisfies you on a personal level and, as such, guarantees your future success. I've learned and witnessed firsthand that when you identify what you are passionate about, you can align that with your gifts, talents and skill set. And when you do, you can successfully:

- Identify what business you will excel at.
- Predict the success of your business.
- Live your calling, purpose and dream.

Whether you want to start a business full-time, supplement your income with a side business, or prepare an exit strategy to escape the cubicle cell or explore the possibilities of entrepreneurship, it is important to know how to connect the dots between your passion and skill set to your business idea.

> *Passion and purpose go hand in hand. When you discover your purpose, you will normally find it's something you're tremendously passionate about."* ~ Steve Pavlina

I simply love what I do professionally and as an entrepreneur; I have the perfect blend of passion, natural skill set fused into my big vision life. Like most women I have come across, I didn't understand what I was gifted with intellectually because it was so natural to me and it didn't seem that big of a deal. But it is a BIG deal! It's interesting how the smallest and simplest things you do can be your greatest gift to the world. When you intertwine your inner vision of how you intentionally want to show up in your life with laser focus, you create a Big Vision! It's really by divine design, passion, vision, and focused intent that I would be doing the work I'm doing today. My *outer vision* circumstance (compromised eyesight) has certainly been the catalyst for me empowering women to move beyond their perceived limitations with courageous confidence to free themselves from the 9-to-5 mindset and start their own passion business. This is my big vision beyond the job! When I experienced my second job layoff in my career, I knew it was time for me to intentionally focus on the vision I had written down in 1997 when I was working as an administrative assistant. It was time for me to start scratching the entrepreneurial itch!

Do you break out in hives thinking about how you can live your entrepreneurial dream while working your full-time job?

If you are really serious and you know in your heart of hearts there is more for you to do beyond your job, whether that is starting your own business, a non-profit organization, or to start a movement, then make sure it fits your personality. When you leap into any type of entrepreneurial venture you must ensure that it's right for you. Is there something that you absolutely love to do? Does it come naturally for you? Do you have the natural skill set for it? These are things you really want to think about because some businesses require different personality traits. For instance, coaching and training is a natural skill set for me: I am a great communicator and I thrive on helping others be their best self. I am approachable, friendly, outgoing, and energetic. I would not thrive in a business where I needed to be logical, analytical, mechanical, and technical. There are some things you will need to learn and some things you can outsource, but it's much better to start a business that you have a natural ability and personality for.

Let's get real, every woman can't wear stilettos. No matter how great they look, they can be hard to walk in, easy to stumble in, and a detriment to your back and feet. If your feet feel better in low comfort shoes, wear them with style. Just like a cute shoe that hurts and doesn't fit or wear properly, a business that doesn't match your natural skill set will cause you pain in the long run. Any business venture will have its ebb and flow in building and growing, but let it be something that you enjoy and don't mind working through the challenging moments of it. Stick to a good fit!

➜ THE DAY JOB AND THE BIG VISION

I bet you wonder where time goes, especially when you wake up and realize another month or year has gone by. You find yourself frustrated because you're on that same unchallenging, dead end, stifling, stress inducing or plateaued job. You feel trapped because your vision is lying dormant inside you. Pursuing your dream doesn't have to be an arduous, complicated or discouraging pursuit; it just requires a little creativity on your part. You go about your day-to-day activities feeling harried and frayed with little energy in the evenings to commit to anything but some peace and quiet time. *"Who has the time or energy to work on a business? Give me a break!"* I can relate whole-heartedly. I remember just waiting to "chill" with a good movie, a glass of wine or watch Lifetime TV in the evenings. However, I had to make a conscious choice to commit to my goals. It's not a criminal act to take a night off sometimes. However, you can always find creative ways to spend time getting what you need done to start your own business one step at a time. If you plan to one day make the exit from being an Employed-preneur to an Entrepreneur, then it's going to take big vision actions and not short comfort thinking.

Every woman doesn't have the luxury or means to quit her day job to pursue her vision as a full-time business owner. Working a part-time or full-time job to build financial resources to make ends meet is a wise thing to do before launching into the deep sea of entrepreneurship without scuba gear. In fact, if your job is in alignment with your vision or is a position that can give you exposure to the right people, experience or visibility in the community, then you are right where you need to be until your appointed time. At times your job may zap the life out of you, but in the meantime it is imperative that you stay motivated to create and live your best life. How can you do this and stay sane too?

Consider some of these strategies you can incorporate into your day. Be aware: It will require you to make some minor adjustments, but remember that it is your dream—You can continue sleeping or wake up and do something about it!

- **Work through your lunch break.** On your dream, of course. Close your door, bring your brown bag from home and get busy. Going to a cozy café or your car works too.

- **Get up an hour earlier.** If you have kids or a spouse, beat them to the punch and carve out a little quiet time to work on your big vision.

- **Skip the evening wine.** For all you wine connoisseurs, I know this is tough, especially for those who need to unwind, but drink water instead. It actually gives you energy, especially in the evenings when things begin to wind down. You need all the energy you can get to work on your vision.

- **Leave when the workday is over.** I haven't seen many people benefit from staying late everyday besides adding more stress, living unbalanced lives, unhappy marriages and illness. If possible, try to negotiate flexible hours.

- **Treat your time as sacred**. Think how many hours you spend watching your favorite show on TV. Now apply that time to your dream with the same level of commitment.

You can come up with your own creative ways to balance work and your big vision. Who said it was going to be easy? It's not, but it can be done.

➜ OVERCOMING THE FAILURE TO LAUNCH SYNDROME

Great ideas can be fun to explore! Starting a new business can seem a bit overwhelming. However, it doesn't have to be with a few simple and doable steps along the way. As a solo-entrepreneur, I've had my own journey of business ventures and new ideas. When I finally found what I am passionate about, the ideas started flowing. I would envision my new business, how it looked and what I looked like in it. Suddenly, it seemed too intimidating to move forward. Then it hit me! I remembered that my mother was an entrepreneur for 35 years and single-handedly started her business on the side before launching it full-time after losing her job. If she could do it successfully without knowing any technology and no marketing strategy back then, surely I could make a go at it with the knowledge I have acquired. So if you are experiencing the *failure to launch* syndrome don't stress. It happens, but you want to get off the launching pad so you can experience the joy of helping those who need what you have to offer in products and or services.

➜ TAKE BABY STEPS AND DO SOMETHING

There's nothing more debilitating than sitting idle on your idea. Even worse, somebody may snatch it and run with it. It can be overwhelming thinking of what to do next. You can do something small and start building from there. Just pick one thing to do and go for it! When I decided to start my coaching business, the first thing I did was research the industry. Second, I interviewed other coaches to figure out my next step. Before I knew it, I was enrolled in coaching school and building my business. It was encouraging to know that I was getting things done in small increments. Relieve yourself from having to have everything perfect. Believe me, you'll find yourself going in circles and not producing any results. Find one thing you can do now and do it, you'll feel really good and be motivated to take the next step.

➜ LEAVE THE PERFECTION TO GOD

It's so easy to get snared by the details of bringing it all together. Yes, you want it to be perfect, but keep it simple. Perfection will drive you nuts! This could possibility lead you down a winding road to nowhere. Here's a simpler way of looking at it: If you want to bake and sell cakes, you could worry about the decorations, the packaging, the delivery, and the marketing. However, your concern *should* be on the cake. The cake is the hallmark of your business. Everything else is secondary. Once you figure out your cake, hold the perfections for the intricate details later, and you'll see that getting started will become easier for you.

➜ TWEAK WHAT'S ALREADY BEEN DONE

You don't have to build from scratch. Look at your competition or a similar business and see what they are doing. All you need is a unique spin, a twist or a better way of delivering what you have to offer. There are no-cost and low-cost ways you can get started. What it boils down to is your branding and unique message for your product and service. Investigate what's out there and see how you can put your unique "seal" on it.

➜ SHARE WITH OTHERS WHAT YOU'RE STARTING

Sometimes people are a little skeptical about telling others their ideas because we've heard horror stories of dream stealers or idea snatchers. Nevertheless, you never know the person you tell just might be the one who can connect you with the right people or resources that could support your idea. I'd encourage you to share with people of influence who have connections and people you meet at networking events. If anything, you get people's interest and they start asking questions. You might get some unique ideas along the way too. Don't be shy—be heard and get the word out! This will help keep you in the entrepreneurial spirit.

➜ ASK FOR WHAT YOU NEED

This relates back to sharing your idea with others. Once you've been sharing your business idea, ask for what you need. If you aren't social media savvy and want to create a presence, ask for a referral. If the people you speak with can't assist you in what you need, ask them for recommendation. You don't have to go at it alone. Here's where networking serves its purpose! You'll be surprised at how much support you will get when you ask for what you need.

Starting your own business doesn't have to be difficult when you have a plan that consists of small consistent steps. You make the decision to how much time you will allot to work on your business. The key is consistency with a plan of action.

Before you know it, you'll be scratching off the small stuff and see your big vision business idea come alive.

Let's sketch out what you see as your ideal business:

- Write down your personal vision. How can you align it with your business idea?

- What do you do that comes so naturally and you just flow in it?

- Is your idea a good match for your personality? Can you see yourself operating in it with love and joy?

- How much time are you willing to invest in your business on a weekly basis?

Let's pull out your calendar and start scheduling in some activities you can do to build your passion business. First, answer these questions to help you see where you can invest a few hours during the evenings/weekends to work on your business:

- Describe the flow of a typical day for you from the time you get up to the time you retire for the evening.

- What part of the day can you devote to working on your business? What activities can you do on those days?

- What systems do you have that can support you in getting things done and staying on track? (i.e. electronic calendar, project management software, apps, etc.)Take some time to write down your ideal activities you would like to happen on a regular basis to build your business.

- Identify three things you are willing to tradeoff to make your big vision a reality?

→ → →

Yeah! You have taken the initial steps in planning how you will spend your time and energy on making your entrepreneurial vision come to life. In the next chapter, we will work on how to invest more into your passion business so you can create the freedom you desire.

FREEDOM NUGGET

Sometimes you may feel like you are slow to learning something new, but don't confuse that with slow to take action.

9

FREEDOM ON INVESTMENT (FOI)

"We are free, truly free, when we don't need to rent our arms to anybody in order to be able to lift a piece of bread to our mouths." ~Ricardo Flores Magon

What is Freedom on Investment (FOI)? Freedom here refers to the power YOU have to take control of your life when you make the proper investment. It comprises any changes you experience in your life that is a result of an investment of money, time, energy, resources, attitude, and mindset it takes in which you, as an investor, receives an investment. Freedom is about not being restrained from making your big vision business idea a reality. If you intend to exit your corporate job to become a full-time entrepreneur, build wealth, create your own economy, supplement your income for a better lifestyle, or develop a cause such as a nonprofit foundation then you'll need an FOI plan of action. This Freedom on Investment (FOI) includes your personal and professional development. Whatever measurement of investment you put in for yourself and in your business idea, you can expect a return. Your FOI equates to you getting what you desire.

When I think about the first time I consciously made the effort to write down my goals for what I desired to achieve professionally, starting a business was one of my long-term goals. Initially, I wanted to pursue a career in human resources and the business idea would come...someday. I can happily say, I've accomplished what I set out to do. I envisioned what I wanted and I got there because I *invested* in my professional development. It has certainly been worth the time, energy, resources, blood, sweat, and tears in getting the degrees I worked so hard for. Investments don't always come cheap and freedom comes at a price. There are tradeoffs and upfront costs, but it yields priceless fruit with the right motive and attitude. You noticed that I said "tradeoffs" and not sacrifices. The word "sacrifice" sounds like you have to punish yourself to have what is divinely yours. Tradeoffs mean you hold off on something and replace it with a new action to get the results you truly desire. That feels betters and it's more empowering too. It's a freedom choice because you're still investing. You honor who you are, your values, your passion, and most importantly, the big vision you hold for your life.

➜ VISION ANNUITY

I have always been an investor in my vision for life. I coined this as my *Vision Annuity*—an investment towards the life I desire to live which entitles me to equal annual payments (accomplished big vision goals). When you invest in yourself and your business, you end up getting paid in the long term for your dedication, diligence and determination. You begin to reap the harvest in your personal and business life.

Investing in yourself and in your business means that each and every time you make a decision to improve your life and the life of others through your products and services, it gets you closer to achieving real success. That's a dividend that keeps on adding up year after year after year! Every investment you put in—whether it's time, energy, money, integrity, and a stick-with-it attitude—you cash in on your FOI. Putting nothing in is a negative against your own Vision Annuity and Freedom on Investment and a debit against your success.

Here are a couple of things you can do to increase your investment status:

1. **Be a bigger player.** Go for the meatier projects or opportunities. It may be a huge investment on the front end, but on the back end, it will generate long-term rewards.

2. **Conquer your fear of technology.** Spend increments of your time learning one new thing that will help you leverage your business.

3. **Don't be bullied by your own excuses.** Maintain your integrity, show up and do what is required for you and the health of your business.

4. **Believe in yourself and the quality of your products/services.** They contribute to your Vision Annuity and a return on your Freedom on Investment.

It's always a plus to do an introspection to identify any negatives towards boosting your Vision Annuity to the investment level you need to enhance yourself and your business.

→ THE JOY AND PAIN OF INVESTMENT

The reason it can feel painful to start a business is simple; it's like giving birth to an elephant. You have this massive idea, a huge desire and passion as big as the Pacific Ocean with a pressing need to control your own destiny. Life is filled with joy and pain, and pain is something you will experience on various levels in life and in business. When you make a decision to give birth to your beautiful idea, you can expect some labor pains just getting the vision out of your head and heart and into the world of anticipating people who need what you have to offer. On top of that, you have to nurture and grow this baby! It can be so much work and joy at the same time. You'll find yourself being stretched and doing things that you may not feel comfortable or adept with such as marketing, networking, collaborating, speaking, planning, and budgeting. There may be times when you question whether or not the investment was really worth it. This is when you revisit the "why" behind your vision. If you desire to one day make an exit from your cubicle or build a sustainable business on the side while working your job, then you'll need to invest in areas that you might not be as strong in as you develop your business.

I initially had many painful events as I was struggling to build my coaching business. I experienced lots of joy in the fact that I was going to be able to help other women create a vision for their life, but the pain of not knowing what first steps to take and having the foundational pieces I needed to attract and get clients caused a lot of frustration. I knew I was trying to figure out most of it on my own. I am a personal development junkie. I'm glancing at my bookshelf as I write this chapter, noticing that all my books are in the self-help category. That probably sounds boring or overkill, but I thrive on personal development. However, when it came time to start building my business, I struggled. And for a while, I was beginning to wonder was it worth it. I realized that trying to do it alone was getting me nowhere and that I needed to invest in a coach to help me create a plan to navigate the roadblocks to reaching my goals. It was the best investment I could have made and I still invest in myself today with a coach and mentor. The joy of investing in my freedom plan is believing I'm worth it and that my *big vision* is a high priority.

➜ UNDERSTAND YOUR "WHY"

You live. You work. You desire a better life, more wealth, more time with family, nice vacations, and to be *freed* from the corporate chains of working for someone else's vision. So what is the true value you place on yourself? What do you want to achieve so that you make a difference in the world? What memories do you want to leave? The biggest question is *why* do you want to start a business? How will it make an impact on you, your family and the people you want to serve? Knowing *why* you want the things you desire is the groundwork for focused intention and consistent contribution to your vision annuity. Your *why* is what you need to propel you forward when all hell breaks loose! It gets you up in the morning ready to take on the day's tasks. It trumps the craziness you have to deal with at work because you have a freedom plan and it gives you the second wind you need when you're threatened with distractions from your big vision plan. Your *why* has high value and anything worth having is worth investing in. How big is your why? How big is your investment?

What do you want freedom *from* and freedom *for*?

If you are struggling with the mindset of staying in Corporate America and want to one day make that leap to work your business full-time, then here are a few things you need to do now.

- Consider other streams of income as a way to build wealth and a sustainable income. Your job shouldn't necessarily be seen as a security blanket.

- Give your vision full attention and the investment it requires.

- Test your idea in the marketplace before taking a full leap.

- Act and think like an entrepreneur while you are an employee.

- Enlist the help of a coach or mentor to get you on the right track with focused action.

- Network with other entrepreneurs and business owners.

This is the preparation for your exit strategy for living your big vision beyond your job. Let your *why* be the reason you invest your time, money, resources, and energy so you can receive the rewards from your Freedom on Investment.

→ MANAGING THE FREEDOM PLAN WHILE WORKING

You find yourself up late at night on the computer, sorting through paperwork, responding to emails, working on a client project, and it seems like you just didn't have enough time to get it all done while you work your job too? I get it! It's not the life of a superwoman, but a committed entrepreneurial woman who wants to get it done. I hear you when you say, "I have so much on my plate and can't seem to balance it with everything else I have to do." You have your business to run, family priorities, community work, and all the things that make life rewarding. If you've been to the time management classes and have implemented all the bells and whistles of technology to help you stay on top of things, then I hope you realize that managing your time is not a skill set; it's a mindset to do it. And more, you have to manage yourself.

Getting sidetracked is a result of not having a plan to tackle your day. I know some of you might like to work on the fly because that's when the creative juices flow. I have learned that when I don't have a plan of action, I will unconsciously meander in all kinds of directions without accomplishing a lot or will create more unfinished projects. The way I managed my business priorities is by having a vision of what I want accomplished in the next three, six, or twelve months. This plan includes my strategies that will help me achieve what I want in my business. When I feel overwhelmed or unaccomplished, I realize that I have not efficiently planned my day.

Here are a few ways you can tackle your day as you build your business as an Employed-preneur:

✓ **Plan your day the night before.** At the end of each day write out all the things you need to do the following day to achieve your goals. The ones you weren't able to complete can be carried over to the next day.

✓ **Prioritize your task.** Number each item and do the dreadful jobs first. Think about how good you'll feel when the dreadful jobs are out of the way and how motivated you'll feel to continue.

✓ **Stick to your task.** Mark off each item as you go, and don't allow yourself to be distracted. I have been notorious for checking e-mails as they come in. I am slowly working on eliminating this habit. Make an agreement with yourself to check for messages every two hours or the best time for you.

✓ **Stop procrastinating.** Procrastination is the thief of time. It's too easy to put things off until another time or until "I've had time to think about it." Do it now!

✓ **Plan your leisure time.** Everyone needs a break to restore, refresh and get rejuvenated. Be aware of those important things that must be done and get them out of the way so you will be more relaxed when it is play time.

✓ **Be real with yourself.** Keep asking, "Is what I'm doing now getting me to where I want to be?" If the answer is no, change what you're doing.

By now, you should know that freedom comes by way of investment. See yourself breaking out and bringing your entrepreneurial vision to life. Your freedom starts with the power to make a conscious decision to do the work it takes to accomplish your goals and big vision for your business. Think of the others you will set free as they benefit from your products or services that you create to make this a better planet for all who need what you have to offer. Give your big vision wings so it can soar. Invest in your freedom plan by investing in YOU!

Are you ready to make the escape to *Freedomland*? Read on to the next chapter.

FREEDOM NUGGET

Consistency and determination will yield the sweetest fruit. You just have to put the work in and patiently wait.

10

THE GREAT ESCAPE

"Never fear a job, always respect it, and always leave yourself a hind door to escape. May your hind door always be open." ~ Red Adair

You understand that the most important thing you can do to have the life you desire is to see yourself where you desire to be. That means creating a vision that unlocks you from the handcuffs of your current reality into the doorway of freedom to have courageous confidence to bring your big vision to life. You no longer have to meander down the dark corridors of your life when you are clear about where you want to be, do and have when you create a vibrant vision that opens the windows to the soul—your inner vision! This radiant light can blind anything that threatens to block your exit strategy that lifts you out of the mundane into the extraordinary life you were created to have on this earth.

Here are three rules to hold onto when you create this magnificent vision:

- **Don't allow someone else's vision be the guidepost for your life.** It's okay to support others with their vision, but PLEASE have your own.

- **Treat and guard your vision like it's the most valued commodity you will ever possess.** Let no one devalue, deface or disparage what you see on the horizon for yourself.

- **Know that your vision is the present and future you.** This is regardless of where you've been, where you've come from, or what you've done in the past.

Visualize what it feels and looks like to be free to create and live your big vision. Close your eyes, feel your hand gently and slowly turning that doorknob and opening the door to your big vision. What's out there waiting for you to step into it? Let's look at how you can get clear on what you see:

What is your big vision?

- Open your mind to the unlimited possibilities for your business and contributions to the world—the people you have a passion to serve.

- Create that *big vision*—a business that honors who you are.

- Explore self-mastery strategies you can use to support your vision.

Here are some foundational components for creating the ideal business you want:

1. ***Who are you? What is your story?***

   What experiences have shaped the person you are today? What problems have you encountered that frustrated, irritated, hurt, or annoyed you? Also, what excites you to make a difference in the world?

2. ***What problem do you want to tackle? And what solution(s) will you provide to combat this problem?***

   The problem/experience you've overcome can be your "why" for your business. Think about what strategies you used to make a transformation in your life and how that can help others do the same.

3. ***What is your mission statement?***

   How will your business serve the greater good?

4. ***Who is your target market or ideal client?***

   What type of client do you see yourself working with? Have you been exposed with or worked with this market before? Why do you want to work with them? Is this a viable market/client, one that can be easily accessed? Where will you go to find them?

You can make the great escape from Pain Island to Pleasure Island, a place that's brimming with unlimited possibilities. You may have the best intentions of doing things differently to make the exit you desire, but there's usually one thing that can cause you to stay hidden behind the door of your freedom plan—not showing up and taking action. My mentor and coach, Catrice M. Jackson, lovingly and unapologetically says, *"Show up, shine and do the damn thing!"* Stop talking and dreaming, hemming and hawing. Show up taking action the best way you can. Catrice is the fire behind my writing this book today. It's been a dream of mine for a very long time, but I had to make the ultimate decision to move on my big goal and open the door to what I wanted to achieve this year. It's that inner vision that I've been talking about in Chapter One to project what you want into reality with focused intention and a plan.

"Being big or small isn't the crucial issue. If you don't move, you don't move." ~ Steve Ballmer

Think about what it's costing you to live behind the closed door of your life. Whatever you aspire to achieve, you must show up and do what you can do to make it happen. I was on a coaching call once with a client of mine and she stated that she was going to be unreasonable. To her, that meant not doing the same things she always did that seemed reasonable. No more staying in the comfort zone and being afraid to show up; she was ready to be recognized for her gifts and things she's never done before. For me, being unreasonable would be moving beyond the status quo in my life and business in a way that will catapult me into the extraordinary woman I am destined to be.

How can you show up?

If you sincerely want to make a shift in your life then you must be an observer of your actions. By being an observer, I mean intentionally monitoring your behavior. Is it lining up with what you say you really want? Good intentions are great. Taking action and doing what you can do with what you have in front of you will get you closer to your big vision. The key to showing up is being consistent in doing what is necessary for any transformation to manifest.

→ SIGNS OF SHOWING UP

- Rising 30 minutes to an hour earlier to work on an aspect of your big vision goals.

- Embracing your fears, but making a decision to take a courageous step anyway.

- Eliminating time wasters that keep you on the couch, watching someone else live their vision.

- Seizing the opportunities with an open mind that will put you in a better position financially, emotionally, physically, and spiritually.

- Recognizing that obstacles are distractions that can be eliminated, minimized, or moved around with an *I can* or *I will* attitude.

You don't have to rid yourself of the fun and joy in your life; no act is too small that it won't make a difference. All you need to do is show up, doing what you can with greater and greater frequency.

If you don't focus on your own life and choose the direction you want to have, you're going to wake up in the morning and life is going to choose that direction for you.

→ ESCAPING THE CAREER AND JOB WAVES

Be innovative, explorative and view your career/job with new eyes. Now is a great time for you to consider creating your own economy. This should be a part of your exit strategy before you decide to make that full leap into entrepreneurship or find yourself in a career transition due to mergers, downsizing, layoff, or sheer burnout.

Here are three things to do to jumpstart your exit strategy:

1. **Shift your gears from the Quiet Zone into the Strike Zone**. Be proactive about your next move and not just "wait it out," be it the economy or just your own fear. The Quiet Zone is a peaceful and comfortable place, but a non-proactive and stagnant one too. You are a remarkable and gifted woman with great ideas. DON'T rest on them! The Strike Zone can be uncomfortable a bit, but that's where the fruit is and it's the only way you are going to gain the confidence you need to pursue the next step you need to take.

2. **Stop competing.** Instead, be yourself. Be unique. When you assess your strengths and skill set, you will be surprised how you can weave your brand or signature into a business concept that will set you apart from what others are doing. Your pain and your triumph could be leading you to your purpose in life. Make it a mission to be authentic; don't fall

prey to being someone other than who you are. Your gifts and talents will make room for you.

3. **Build strong networks and alliances.** There's one thing for sure: As women, we know how to gather and socialize. We host parties at our homes, family reunions, facilitate meetings—you name it and we can pull it off. You can use those same skills in building business relationships. Let people know what you are doing and what you're looking for as you are developing your business. Find diverse groups to be a part of and make some connections. Someone may hold the key to what you need to jumpstart your business venture.

In the classic book, *The Science of Getting Rich* by Wallace Wattles, he states, "There is an abundance of opportunity for the man [woman] who will go with the tide instead of trying to swim against it." If you have positioned yourself in a box, come out and enter the Strike Zone. No more swimming against the tide (fear, lack of confidence, and comfort zone). Be free and ride the waves of success as you are creating your own current.

➜ YOUR COMFORT ZONE IS A TRAP

I am going to give you some bittersweet advice: If you want more success than you have today in life or in your business, you will have to shake things up a little more and leave your cushy, perceived-to-be-safe comfort zone. Breathe. Comfort zones feel safe and give the illusion that you're in control. Life appears, in our comfort zone, relatively familiar and stable which is contradictory to growth. One of my favorite books is *Who Moved My Cheese!* This simple and short read demonstrates what happens when you make a decision to leave from the familiar to an unknown place in life. And that unknown place can be full of surprises, opportunities, abundance, and wealth waiting for you. When I was in a career transition, I quickly learned that I had to leave my comfort zone if I wanted to be in control of my own destiny. I began the journey by taking risk, criticism, disappointment, failure, looking foolish, and trying new things. To this day, I remain committed to the process of developing the courage to rise above the ordinary and escape my comfort trap. I made the decision not to continue pursuing small and unassuming positions or roles for rest of my life and career. I had a tugging on my heart that was saying that there was something else for me to do and I was becoming too comfortable in those roles, yet wanting more for myself. Playing small was no longer an option for me, I chose a career that would put me in the spotlight (something that I have always shied away from) that showcases my passion, purpose and big vision that I've held for myself. I've taken leaps of faith into unknown territory. It has been a blessing and the joy of my life! Don't let your comfort zone be a trap.

Here's why:

- It's designed to stunt your growth and development.

- It will keep you looking back, wishing and waiting.

- It crushes your self-esteem and confidence.

- It will keep you from living out your purpose and your dream, and all the splendor of life!

Breaking out of any situation or circumstance for a better you and a better life isn't always easy, but it's doable. I'm doing it and you can too! Great escapes, sometimes takes practice until you can get enough traction to make bigger and bolder tracks. You may have gotten comfortable with your life, but you are unhappy, disenchanted or frustrated with your current reality. The good news is that you can remodel your reality with a new vision that showcases your divine greatness.

➜ FOUR PRINCIPLES FOR A SUCCESSFUL EXIT

You may have a different definition for success based on how you see it, experience it or perceive it. Success isn't based on your economic status, your position or social presence; it's how you choose to live your life. Earl Nightingale, in *The Strangest Secret,* states, *"Success is the progressive realization of a worthy ideal. If someone is working toward a predetermined goal, and knows where he or she is going, that person is a success."* The most successful people are the ones who are disciplined and determined about what they want for themselves and the people around them. When you intentionally set your sights on achieving a specific goal to attain your big vision and you accomplish it, then you are a success. Successful people don't wait for life to just happen. They do whatever is in their power to do. You can fire up your success outlook with: Vision + Plan = Success.

Following these four principles will help you put a plan in motion to successfully bring your big vision to life:

1. **Know your WHY.** What do you want and why do you want it? Create a vision board if you need to help you stay

focused. Write it down clearly and post it where it is visible. When times get tough, you need something that will remind you *why* you are doing this.

2. **Take personal responsibility and make a commitment.** Own your role in creating the life/business that you want. You and only you decide what you can do and will do to make your life better. Choose what you can do today and stick with it. If you don't commit to doing the things that will enhance your life, you will continue to move in circles.

3. **Start living the life you envisioned.** Come out of the gate and stop waiting. No more hiding behind what you don't have or what isn't right. Work with what's in front of you. Grab hold to the big vision and not the day-to-day nuisance.

4. **Be true to yourself.** You don't have to compare yourself to what others are doing. You were created for a unique purpose, so let your originality shine through.

Whatever your aim is in life, do it with intention and follow through. You are so close to having your big vision come to life. All you need to do is open the door and walk through it with courageous confidence to do the work to make it your new reality.

I dare you to push the door and grab what is your birthright. You were created for something great beyond your perceived limitations and current status. **Be bold, be brave** and **be the creator of your destiny**. It's your exit door to freedom to live your big vision life!

ABOUT THE AUTHOR

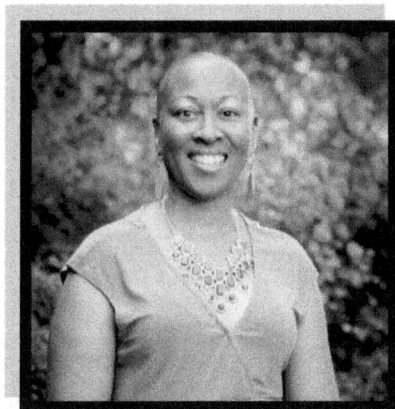

Cherri Walston is the founder of Big Vision Biz, LLC a coaching business helping working women start their passion business. She is also an Inspiration Speaker, Trainer and Visionary Entrepreneur.

Entrepreneurial women who found themselves stifled and held back by Corporate America are singing the praises of Cherri Walston, *The Big Vision Mentor*. They are reenergized, focused, and determined to start, build, and grow their very own **successful business that's divinely suited for them**.

Cherri is very skillful at helping professional women articulate their passionate life's vision. She also leads them to create a soul-fulfilling business that aligns with their personal mission. Cherri is **compassionate, empathetic, and knows your struggles** because she has faced them herself and has overcome them. She discovered she had a natural gift of helping women transform their lives.

For the past 15 years, **Cherri has worked in the Training and Development field as a trainer** for a world-class hospital, manufacturing company and a major network marketing company. She started her personal coaching business, eventually deciding to focus on entrepreneurial women who wanted to start their own business, but are unclear on where to begin and what steps to take to achieve consistent income.

Cherri is always excited and prepared to share her secret discovery with women so they can achieve their personal business dreams. Today, Cherri is spreading her wings and implementing her divinely-right blueprint to inspire hundreds of other entrepreneurial women to start, build, and grow a successful and inspired business they will love.

Cherri received her Masters of Science Degree in Adult Education from North Carolina A&T State University and a Professional Coaching Certification from Coach Training Alliance.

Cherri currently lives in Greensboro, NC and enjoys traveling and playing golf.

**You can contact Cherri via email at
cherriwalston@gmail.com**

/ bigvisionmentor   **@bigvisionmentor**

www.ingramcontent.com/pod-product-compliance
Lightning Source LLC
LaVergne TN
LVHW051249080426
835513LV00016B/1815